日本語・英語解説による
続・言語活動成功事例集

藤井昌子／スティーヴン・アシュトン 共著

Communication Activities

開隆堂

は　じ　め　に

　教師であれば誰でも、「今日の授業はうまくいった」という喜びを味わいたいものです。授業がうまくいった日は心は軽やかですし、反対に授業のうまくいかなかった日は心が重くなります。授業がうまくいくかどうかは、どれだけ授業の準備をしたかと深く関連します。「教材研究をじっくりやって授業に臨みたい」というのがすべての教師の切実な願いでしょう。にもかかわらず、実際には行事や会議、生徒指導、部活動などに忙殺され、授業準備にほとんど時間をかけられないのが教師の実情です。忙しい教師でも、モデルになるような教材や展開例がどこかにストックされていて、いつでもアクセスできたらどんなにか助かるだろう。そんな思いから本書は生まれました。

　本書は3年前に発刊した『言語活動成功事例集—Communication Activities』の続編になりますが、内容が難しくなっているわけではありません。もちろん、活動内容は前回のものとすべて異なりますが、レベル的には前回の事例集とほぼ同程度のものを意識しました。

　また、前回と同様に説明を日本語と英語の2本立てにしました。ALTとのティームティーチングを意識してのことです。日本人教師が英語の説明を読んで言語活動をイメージするのは大変なことですし、同様にALTが日本語の説明を理解するのも大変なことです。この本を見れば、日本人教師とALTが同時に活動の内容を理解できるようにしました。もちろん、すべての活動例は日本人教師単独の授業でも使えることは言うまでもありません。また「成功」という文字が示すように、すべての活動は授業で実際に行われ、うまく展開したものを元にしています。さらに、活動を行なう際に気をつけるべき点について「ひとことコーナー」で触れました。授業で実施するとなれば、「こうすれば、うまくいく」「こうすると、まずい」という経験に根ざしたワンポイント・アドバイスが一番役に立つと思ったからです。

　とはいえ、本書に書かれている展開例はあくまでもモデルに過ぎません。目の前の生徒の実態に合わせてお使いください。また、新しい学習指導要領では「言語の使用場面と働き」という用語が繰り返し述べられてます。どのような場面で、どのような働きをすることば(英語)が使われるのかをよく考え、本書の活動例を工夫してお使いください。

　たくさんの実践例を紹介してくださった先生方、ありがとうございました。

　また、本書の英語の部分の執筆を担当してくれた英国出身のSteven Ashtonにもお礼を申し上げます。彼は一昨年まで埼玉県立総合教育センターのALTとして活躍し、現在はELECで教材開発や教員研修を担当しております。彼からもたくさんの実践例を頂きました。

　最後に、この本が全国の先生方の毎日の授業に少しでもお役に立つことを、心から願っております。

2001年　夏

藤井　昌子

Preface

Do you remember your very first lesson? I remember mine. September 1997. Forty Japanese students and one Japanese teacher of English in the classroom, all looking at me. Hiding my nervousness well, I went ahead with my self-introduction. Although surprised at the shyness of the students, I thought, at the time, that my first lesson as a professional teacher had been rather good. It was over the course of the next week or so that I came to realize that perhaps it wasn't quite so satisfactory, after all. One of my colleagues, for example, pointed out that it was me, rather than the students, who was doing most of the talking. So, I made changes to my lesson plan, and my self-introduction evolved into a more communicative, educational and enjoyable experience for the students, my Japanese team-teaching colleagues and for me. I learned a lot from this, and in subsequent oral communication classes I always tried to achieve three aims: to give my students a lot of opportunities to speak to each other, to teach them something worthwhile, and to let them have fun.

In this book, Mrs Fujii and I have collected together some teaching ideas for communicative, educational and enjoyable lessons. Some of the ideas are ours, many have been contributed by fellow teachers, while others still are old favorites. Very many students have enjoyed learning English through the activities upon which this book is based, and we're sure yours will too.

I was delighted when Mrs Fujii asked me to work with her on this project, the follow-up to the very successful book she wrote with Ivan Berkel. Her energy and enthusiasm have been an inspiration! I've enjoyed the experience immensely, so thank you, Mrs Fujii!

Mrs Fujii and I are very grateful to all the teachers who so generously shared their lesson plans, ideas and materials with us, and to all the unknown creators of the old favorites, the origins of which are lost in time! I'm sure my mother, Alice, will be surprised to find her name here, but Mum did a lot of research on some of the activities: this is just to say I appreciate it! It's also a pleasure to thank my "geat beat" friend (sorry, a private joke), Yukari Yamaguchi, for her support and assistance.

When I'm trying out a new idea in class, I never get everything right first time. A lot of students are subjected to my trial runs and experimentation. So a big hand to all my students for their patience and feedback, and for all the pleasure they gave me! If they learned only half as much from me as I did from them, I think I've achieved something worthwhile!

When you use activities from this book, always demonstrate to the students what you want them to do, rather than explaining it to them. The simplest activities, when set out only in words, can take on frightening complexity. Take a moment, for example, to think how you might instruct someone to tie their shoelaces in words only—no demonstration, drawing or gestures allowed. See what I mean? Another advantage that demonstration offers is that students don't have to sit through lengthy explanations in Japanese. So before class, think how you can best demonstrate or role play the instructions. Your students will understand what they're supposed to be doing much more clearly, they'll learn more, and hopefully come to enjoy English a little better too!

Good luck!

Steven Ashton
August, 2001

CONTENTS

はじめに／Preface　3
活動目的一覧表　8

1. Find Three Students ……………………………………………… 10
クラスの中で役割の異なる3人を探し出す
Students practice a simple dialogue and identify who is playing a different role.

2. Code Breaker ……………………………………………………… 12
コード表を用いて，聞き取った数字をアルファベットになおす
Students decipher series of numbers into words or sentences.

3. Calendar …………………………………………………………… 16
月や曜日の名前を使ってのフルーツ・バスケット
Students practice the names of the months and days of the week.

4. Grab It! ……………………………………………………………… 18
カルタとりの要領で現在進行形を学ぶ
Using picture cards, students practice the present progressive tense.

5. Dot to Dot ………………………………………………………… 22
数字と数字を結んで現れてくる絵はどんな絵？
Students practice numbers by describing and drawing straight-line pictures.

6. Which Hand Is the Dog In? …………………………………… 26
「どちらの手に犬がいますか」指定した動物のカードを持っている方の手を当てる
By using a simple dialogue, students practice the names of animals.

7. Find the Missing Letter ………………………………………… 30
読まれた語の不足している文字や余分な文字を探す
Students try to find missing or extra letters in words read aloud by the teacher.

8. How Do I Look? ………………………………………………… 32
相手のジェスチャーがどのような気分・気持ちを表そうとしているのか当てる
Students act out their feelings and practice the vocabulary of emotions.

9. Let's Play Cards! ………………………………………………… 36
カルト取りの要領でヒントに合う単語カードを探す
Students compete to choose word cards that match hints read out by the teacher.

10. Who Am I? ……………………………………………………… 40
自分の背中に貼られた人物は誰か，質問しながら推測していく
By asking questions, students guess the secret identity they have been given.

11. Name the Animal ……………………………………………… 44
比較級を使って，相手が思い浮かべている動物を推測していく
Using comparative sentences, students guess the names of animals.

12. Q&A Maze Game ········ 48
すごろくゲームで，日常生活の表現を定着させる
Using a board game format, students familiarize themselves with useful daily expressions.

13. Making Words ········ 52
ある単語の文字を組み替えて，できるだけたくさんの単語を作る
Students make words from the constituent letters of a given word.

14. Rows and Columns ········ 54
縦列・横列が交互に起立し，すばやく質問に答える
An exciting, rapid-fire quiz game.

15. Dash Off the Answer ········ 62
チーム対抗の早押しクイズゲーム
Students review target grammar and key expressions through a fast-moving team game.

16. What Do You See? ········ 70
絵やポスターのなかに見たものを英語で表現する
Students describe a picture or poster.

17. Concentration ········ 72
一連の動作をする間に，指示された語を言う
An elimination game in which students try to think of as many words for given categories as possible.

18. Interviewing the ALT ········ 74
グループで ALT に質問する
Groups interview the ALT and then quiz the class.

19. Speaking Competition ········ 76
短い英文を作り，できるだけ早く発表する
Students compete to make sentences that practice target grammar or key expressions.

20. Find the Whole Story ········ 80
聞いた話をできるだけ正確に再現する
Groups of students compete to write a story they have just heard.

21. Some Tips for Reading Aloud ········ 82
音読を成功に導くあの手この手
Techniques to overcome students' reluctance to read aloud in class.

22. Let's Be a Cartoonist! ① ········ 86
4コママンガのセリフを英語に訳す
Students translate comic strips into English.

23. Let's Be a Cartoonist! ② ········ 90
マンガを見て，それにふさわしいセリフを英語で書く
Students create their own dialogues for simple comic strips.

24. What's Happened? ········ 92
2枚の絵の間に起こったことを想像して英語で書く
Students imagine what has taken place between a "before" and "after" picture.

25. **Who's Who ?** 94
   手がかりをもとに絵の中の人物が誰かを特定する
   By piecing together clues, students identify the seven people in a picture.

26. **Look！ I'm on TV！** 98
   テレビコマーシャルを作り発表する
   Groups of students act out their own television commercials for everyday objects.

27. **Repairing Broken Sentences** 102
   カードにあるキーワードを用いて相手に質問する
   Students have simple conversations, beginning with a question made up from keywords.

28. **Who's My Special Friend ?** 104
   このカードは誰についての情報か，質問をして当てる
   Using anonymous personal information, students track down their Special Friends.

29. **What Do You Think ?** 108
   トピックカードに書かれた文をきっかけにグループで会話を続ける
   Students have free conversation or discussion prompted by particular topics.

30. **Balloon Game** 112
   1人気球から飛び降りないと全員が助からない…，飛び降りる人は誰？
   Students practice some debating skills in this survival game.

31. **Simple Pair Debate** 114
   ペアで好き嫌いの理由を述べ合う
   Students give reasons for liking or disliking certain topics.

32. **Brainstorm** 116
   ある命題について賛成・反対の理由をできるだけ多く考える
   Students brainstorm to make arguments for and against a given proposition.

  参考文献 121
  おわりに／Afterword 122
  執筆協力者 124

活動目的一覧表

No.	Activity	Level	Purpose					
			L	S	R	W	I.C.	Others
1	Find Three Students	初級		○				慣用表現
2	Code Breaker	初級	◎		○			Numbers
3	Calendar	初級〜中級	○					Vocabulary
4	Grab It!	初級	○					Grammar
5	Dot to Dot	初級	○	○			○	Numbers
6	Which Hand Is the Dog In?	初級		○			○	Vocabulary
7	Find the Missing Letter	初級〜中級	○					Spelling
8	How Do I Look?	初級〜中級	○	◎			○	感情表現
9	Let's Play Cards!	初級〜中級	○					Vocabulary
10	Who Am I?	初級〜上級		○			○	
11	Name the Animal	初級〜中級	○	◎			◎	Grammar
12	Q&A Maze Game	初級〜中級	◎	○		○		
13	Making Words	初級〜中級						Vocabulary
14	Rows and Columns	初級〜上級	◎	○				
15	Dash Off the Answer	初級〜中級	◎			○		Grammar
16	What Do You See?	初級〜中級	○	◎				
17	Concentration	初級〜上級	○	○				Vocabulary
18	Interviewing the ALT	初級〜中級	○	○		○		異文化理解
19	Speaking Competition	初級〜中級	○	◎	○	○		Grammar
20	Find the Whole Story	初級〜上級	◎			○		
21	Some Tips for Reading Aloud	初級〜上級	○	○	◎			
22	Let's Be a Cartoonist! ①	中級〜上級		○		◎		
23	Let's Be a Cartoonist! ②	中級〜上級		○		◎		
24	What's Happened?	中級〜上級		○		◎		
25	Who's Who?	中級〜上級	○	◎	○	○	○	
26	Look! I'm on TV!	中級〜上級	◎	◎		○		
27	Repairing Broken Sentences	中級〜上級	○	◎			◎	
28	Who's My Special Friend?	初級〜中級	◎	◎		○	◎	
29	What Do You Think?	中級〜上級	◎	○		◎		
30	Balloon Game	中級〜上級	◎	◎		○	◎	Debate
31	Simple Pair Debate	中級〜上級	○	◎			○	Debate
32	Brainstorm	上級	◎	◎			◎	Debate

Usage			
WU	Prac.	Rev.	Others
	○	○	
○	○	○	
	○	○	
	○	○	
	○	○	
	○	○	
		○	
○	○	○	
		○	定期試験後
			定期試験後
	○	○	
	○	○	
○			定期試験後
○		○	
	○	○	
○			
○			定期試験後
			定期試験後
	○	○	
			定期試験後
	○		
			定期試験後
			定期試験後
			定期試験後
			定期試験後
			定期試験後
○	○	○	
	○		
	○		
	○		
	○		
	○		

本書で取り上げた活動事例は，ほぼレベル順に配列してあります。実際の授業で行う際には左の表を参考にして，その活動がどの領域に焦点を当てたものであるか，また，授業のどのような場面に適しているかなどを確認した上で，目的に合った活動を選ぶようにしてください。

★　　★　　★

When selecting an activity, please refer to this chart. Because the level of activities in this book ranges from easy to difficult, we recommend taking the time to find activities that match your students' level and complement the accompanying lesson. This chart will help you better understand which aspect of communication is emphasized in each activity. Additionally, this chart indicates the portion of the lesson for which the activity may be most effective.

略号

L: Listening

S: Speaking

R: Reading

W: Writing

I.C.: Interactive Communication

WU: Warm-up

Prac.: Practice

Rev.: Review

ACTIVITY 1

Find Three Students

クラスの中で互いに質問し合いながら，他の生徒と役割の違う3人を探していく。目標文の定着を目指す活動。

Level: 初級
Purpose: Speaking／慣用表現(Sure.／Sorry, I can't.)の定着
Materials: 慣用表現を書いた小さな紙(生徒数分)
Usage: 授業の中での活動，復習
Time: 準備—10分　　活動—10分

● Description of Activity ●

1. 下のように，手伝いを頼む母または父と子どもの対話を黒板に書き，生徒に隣の席同士でペアを組ませて十分に対話練習させる。
   Mom/Dad: Help me in the kitchen, please.
   Child: Sure.／Sorry, I can't.
2. 活動について次のように説明する。
   「みなさんはこれから教室を歩き回って相手を見つけ対話練習をします。子どもの役をするときは，この後みなさんに配る小さな紙に書かれてあるとおりに，"Sure." または "Sorry, I can't." と答えてください。"Sorry, I can't." と書いた紙は3枚あります。できるだけたくさんの友達と対話しましょう。言うことを聞かない子，つまり "Sorry, I can't." と答える子が3人見つかったら，先生のところに言いに来てください。」
3. "Sure." または "Sorry, I can't." と書いてある小さな紙を，1枚ずつ裏向きにして生徒に配る。
4. 活動開始。生徒は教室を歩き回って相手を見つけ，役割を交替しながら対話練習する。3人を見つけた生徒は教師に報告し，自分の席に座る。ただし，"Sorry, I can't." のカードを持った生徒はそうせずに，他の生徒のために活動を続ける。
5. 席に着いた生徒が10人ほどになったら活動を終了する。

ひとことコーナー

- 生徒に配る紙を用意する時間がない場合は，生徒全員に目を閉じさせ，3人の生徒の肩をポンと叩き，目を開けさせて「肩をたたかれた人は『言うことを聞かない子』になってね」と言えば，簡単に活動を行うことができる。
- この活動は単純であるが，生徒にとっては「宝探し」や「犯人探し」のような楽しい活動になる。
- この活動はさまざまな表現の定着に応用できるので，中・上級レベルでも使うことができる。例えば，
  ① "Shall we ～?" "Yes, let's."／"No, thank you." を定着させたい時
   A: Shall we eat sushi?
   B: Yes, let's.／No, thank you. (3人のみ)
  ② "Do you know ～?" "Yes, I do."／"Sorry, I don't." を定着させたい時
   A: Excuse me, please, but do you know where the station is?
   B: Yes, I do.／Sorry, I don't. (3人のみ)

1. Find Three Students

★ ★ ★

> **Students practice a dialogue which contains target language with their classmates. They try to find the three students who have been assigned a different role to the rest of the class.**
>
> **Level:** Beginner
> **Purpose:** Speaking / Useful expressions (Sure. / Sorry, I can't.)
> **Materials:** Small slip of paper for each student
> **Usage:** Practice, Review
> **Time:** *Preparation* —10 minutes   *Activity* —10 minutes

● **Description of Activity** ●

1. Write the following dialogue between Mom or Dad and their child on the board and have the students make pairs with their neighbors and practice it:
   Mom/Dad: Help me in the kitchen, please.
      Child: Sure. / Sorry, I can't.

2. Demonstrate the activity.
   "You are going to walk around the class and find a student to practice the dialogue with. When you play the role of the child, you must reply "Sure" or "Sorry, I can't" according to the small slip of paper that I will give to each of you later. There are three slips that say "Sorry, I can't"; all the others say "Sure." Practice the dialogue with many other students. As soon as you know the names of the three students who cannot help Mom or Dad, come and tell me."

3. Distribute the "Sure" and "Sorry, I can't" slips of paper, face down, to each student.

4. Start the activity. Students walk around the class, pairing off and practicing the dialogue with each other. As soon as students know who the three are, they tell the teacher and then sit down on their own seats, except in the case of those who have the "Sorry, I can't" cards; they continue with the activity.

5. Once ten students are sitting, the activity is over.

Additional Information

- If there is not sufficient time in which to prepare the slips of paper, have all the students close their eyes and pat three of them on the shoulder. Ask them to open their eyes and say, "I patted three students on the shoulder. They are the three students who cannot help."
- Although this activity is very simple, for the students it is like a "treasure hunt" or "playing detectives," and, as such, is a lot of fun.
- This activity can be used to practice many types of expressions, even with more advanced students. See examples (p.10).

ACTIVITY 2

Code Breaker

読み上げられた数字を素早く書き取り,それをコード・キーを使って単語や文に解読していく活動。

Level: 初級
Purpose: Listening, Reading／数字
Materials: ワークシート
Usage: ウォームアップ,授業中での活動,復習
Time: 準備―5分　活動―5〜15分

● Description of Activity ●

1. 生徒全員にワークシート(p.14参照)を配る。
2. 教師は次のように指示する。
   「これから数字を読み上げますので,その数字をワークシートに書き取りなさい。次に,今配ったワークシートにあるコード・キーを使って,その数字をアルファベットに解読していきます。解読できた人は大きな声で答えを言ってください。」
3. 活動開始。あらかじめ用意したリスト(p.15, Example Code List 参照)の数字を読み上げる。
4. 生徒は聞き取った数字をワークシートに書き取り,コード・キーを見ながらアルファベットに直して単語や文を作る。答えがわかった生徒は大きな声で解読した語や文を叫ぶ。
5. 3,4の活動を適当な回数繰り返す。

Code Key

1	2	3	4	5	6	7	8	9	10
A	B	C	D	E	F	G	H	I	J
11	12	13	14	15	16	17	18	19	20
K	L	M	N	O	P	Q	R	S	T
21	22	23	24	25	26	27	28	29	30
U	V	W	X	Y	Z	,	.	?	!

- hello　　　　　　　8-5-12-12-15
- Thank you.　　　　20-8-1-14-11　25-15-21-28

ひとことコーナー

・この活動は英語の数字を聞き取ることが目的ではあるが,同時に単語や文を認識する活動にもなる。しかも,英語を学び始めの生徒にとってはとても楽しい活動になる。

2. Code Breaker

★　　★　　★

Students write down a series of numbers read out by the teacher. Using Code Keys, they transform the sequence into a word or sentence.

Level: Beginner
Purpose: Listening, Reading／Numbers
Materials: Worksheet
Usage: Warm-up, Practice, Review
Time: *Preparation*—5 minutes　　*Activity*—5 to 15 minutes

● Description of Activity ●

1. Distribute a worksheet (see p.14) to each student.
2. Demonstrate the activity.
   "I will say some numbers. Write them down on your worksheets. Then match the numbers to the letters using the Code Keys. When you can read the message, say it aloud!"
3. Start the activity. Read out a list of numbers prepared before the class (see Example Code List, p.15).
4. Students write the numbers down on their worksheets and transform the sequence into a word or sentence using the Code Keys. The student who deciphers the word or sentence first calls it out.
5. Repeat the procedure in steps 3 and 4 as often as desired.

Additional Information

- The main aim of this activity is to give students practice in listening to and understanding numbers. At the same time, however, it is good for teaching students to recognize words and sentences. For beginners, it is a lot of fun.

Worksheet

Code Breaker

Class _____ Name _____

Code Key

1	2	3	4	5	6	7	8	9	10
A	B	C	D	E	F	G	H	I	J
11	12	13	14	15	16	17	18	19	20
K	L	M	N	O	P	Q	R	S	T
21	22	23	24	25	26	27	28	29	30
U	V	W	X	Y	Z	,	.	?	!

1. _____

2. _____

3. _____

4. _____

5. _____

2. Code Breaker

Example Code List

1. eye   5-25-5
2. and   1-14-4
3. book   2-15-15-11
4. school   19-3-8-15-15-12
5. English   5-14-7-12-9-19-8
6. sister   19-9-19-20-5-18
7. teacher   20-5-1-3-8-5-18
8. morning   13-15-18-14-9-14-7
9. Saturday   19-1-20-21-18-4-1-25
10. January   10-1-14-21-1-18-25
11. Thank you.   20-8-1-14-11   25-15-21-28
12. Happy birthday!   8-1-16-16-25   2-9-18-20-8-4-1-25-30
13. I like sport.   9   12-9-11-5   19-16-15-18-20-28
14. I have a dog.   9   8-1-22-5   1   4-15-7-28
15. Mary is a student.   13-1-18-25   9-19   1   19-20-21-4-5-14-20-28
16. Can Tom speak French?   3-1-14   20-15-13   19-16-5-1-11   6-18-5-14-3-8-29
17. Do you play soccer?   4-15   25-15-21   16-12-1-25   19-15-3-3-5-18-29
18. How old are you?   8-15-23   15-12-4   1-18-5   25-15-21-29
19. What day is it tomorrow? 23-8-1-20   4-1-25   9-19   9-20
                             20-15-13-15-18-18-15-23-29
20. Where does Ken live?   23-8-5-18-5   4-15-5-19   11-5-14   12-9-22-5-29

ACTIVITY 3

Calendar

> フルーツ・バスケットの要領で，月や曜日の名前を定着させる活動。

Level: 初級～中級
Purpose: Listening／Vocabulary
Materials: 「月」カード，「曜日」カード（それぞれ生徒と教師数分）
Usage: 授業の中での活動，復習
Time: 準備—15分　　活動—10～30分

● Description of Activity ●

1. 机を教室の後ろに移動させ，空いたスペースに椅子を並べて１つの大きな輪を作らせる。教師の１人には椅子がなく，輪の中央に立っている。他の人は椅子に座る。
2. 生徒全員に，月の名前を書いたカードと曜日の名前を書いたカードを各１枚ずつ配布する。教師も同様に２種類のカードを持つ。
3. 活動について説明する。
   ①鬼は輪の中央に立ち，ある月の名前（例えば"April"）か曜日の名前（例えば"Thursday"）を１つ言う。
   ②鬼が言ったカードを持っている人は全員，すぐに別の椅子に移動しなければならない。この時，自分の隣の席に移動してはならない。
   ③鬼も椅子に座ろうとするので，椅子に座れない人が１人出る。その人が次の鬼になる。
4. 輪の中央にいる教師が最初の鬼となり，活動を開始する。３の活動を時間がくるまで続ける。

ひとことコーナー

- この活動は，以下のように鬼が出す指示を工夫することで，変化をつけることができる。
  ①月の名前を一度に２つ（または３つ）言う。
  ②曜日の名前を一度に２つ（または３つ）言う。
  ③月と曜日の名前を１つずつ（２つずつ，または３つずつ）言う。
  ④"Calendar"の合図で全員が動く。ただし，この命令は控えめに。
  鬼が月や曜日の名前を２つ以上言ったときは，どちらか１つでもそのカードを持っていたら，席を移動しなければならない。

3. Calendar

★　　　★　　　★

> **Using the fruit basket format, students practice the names of the months and days of the week.**
>
> **Level:** Beginner to Intermediate
> **Purpose:** Listening/Vocabulary
> **Materials:** Month and day of the week card for each student and teacher
> **Usage:** Practice, Review
> **Time:** *Preparation*—15 minutes　　*Activity*—10 to 30 minutes

● **Description of Activity** ●

1. Move the desks to the back of the class. Arrange the chairs in a large circle. Everyone sits except for one of the teachers, who has no chair and stands in the middle of the circle.
2. Distribute one month and one day of the week card to each participant—the students and teachers.
3. Demonstrate the activity.
   ①The person who stands in the middle of the circle is "It." "It" says the name of a month, like April, or a day of the week, like Thursday.
   ②Everyone who has the corresponding card must move to another chair. Participants cannot move to the chairs immediately adjacent to them.
   ③"It" also tries to sit on a chair, so one person will not be able to sit. This person is the new "It."
4. The teacher standing in the middle of the circle is the first "It." Start the activity. Follow the procedure in step 3 and continue until time runs out.

Additional Information

- This activity can be varied in many ways. For example:
  ①"It" can call out the names of two/three months at a time.
  ②"It" can call out the names of two/three days of the week at a time.
  ③"It" can call out a month and a day of the week (two/three months and two/three days).
  ④"It" can call out "Calendar!" to make all the students move. This command should be used sparingly, however.

  When more than one word is called out, students holding any of the corresponding cards must move.

ACTIVITY 4

Grab It !

読まれた現在進行形の文を表している絵カードを，カルタとりの要領でとり合う活動。

Level: 初級
Purpose: Listening／現在進行形の定着
Materials: カルタシート，はさみ
Usage: 授業中での活動，復習
Time: 準備—5分　　活動—30分

● **Description of Activity** ●

1. 生徒に隣の席同士でペアを組ませ，机を移動して向い合わせに座らせる。
2. 生徒全員に Grab It! シート (pp.20-21参照) を配る。
3. それぞれの絵が表している現在進行形の文を，英語で正確に発音できるように練習する。
4. 各ペアにどちらか一方の Grab It! シートの絵カードをはさみで切り取らせる。
5. 活動開始。各ペアは机の上にカード20枚を並べ，教師が読んだ文を表している絵カードをとり合う。カードを多くとったほうが勝ちとなる。

ひとことコーナー
・ペアでの活動の他，4人グループで行うこともできる。この場合，それぞれがとり合っても，2人ずつのチーム対抗戦にしてもよい。さらに，カードは2人または3人分(40枚または60枚)使うとよい。

4. Grab It!

★   ★   ★

The teacher reads out sentences in the present progressive tense. The students compete to grab the matching picture cards.

Level:	Beginner
Purpose:	Listening/Use of the present progressive
Materials:	Grab It! sheet for each pair of students, Scissors
Usage:	Practice, Review
Time:	*Preparation*—5 minutes *Activity*—30 minutes

● Description of Activity ●

1. Have the students make pairs with one of their neighbors. Have each pair move their desks to sit face to face.
2. Distribute a Grab It! sheet (see pp. 20-21) to each student.
3. Let the students practice the pronunciation of the present progressive sentences that match the pictures.
4. Have the students in each pair cut out all of the picture cards from one of the Grab It! sheets.
5. Start the activity. Each pair scatters the 20 cards onto the desk, face up. The teacher reads out a sentence in the present progressive and each student tries to take the matching card. The student who takes the most cards wins.

Additional Information

- This activity can also be undertaken in groups of four: either four students acting independently, or as two teams of two. In such cases, two or three sets of cards (so 40 or 60 cards in all) should be used.

Grab It! Sheet

※発音練習する時は，必ずp.20とp.21を切り離してお使いください。

20

① The woman is waiting at the station.	⑤ He's cooking dinner.	⑨ She's eating an orange.	⑬ The animals are learning English.	⑰ The elephant is riding the bicycle.
② The student is asking a question.	⑥ The dolphin is crying.	⑩ The horse is singing a song.	⑭ She's opening the door.	⑱ They're smiling.
③ They're building a house.	⑦ The dog is drawing a cat.	⑪ The girl is helping her father.	⑮ They're playing in the garden.	⑲ She's swimming in the sea.
④ The girl is carrying some books.	⑧ The bird is drinking water.	⑫ They're holding hands.	⑯ It's raining.	⑳ The men are walking in the park.

※ Before practicing the pronunciation, separate pages 20 and 21.

ACTIVITY 5

Dot to Dot

一面に数字のついた点が並んでいるシートに，読み上げられた数字と数字とを線で結びながら絵を描いていく活動。

Level: 初級
Purpose: Listening, Speaking／数字
Materials: ピクチャーグリッド（出題用のものと提示用に拡大コピーしたもの），
ナンバーグリッド（各生徒に5枚ずつ）
Usage: 授業の中での活動，復習
Time: 準備—5～10分　　活動—30～50分

● **Description of Activity** ●

1. 生徒全員にナンバーグリッド（p.24参照）を配る。生徒にピクチャーグリッド（p.25参照）を見られないようにしながら，教師が読み上げる数字の点と点とを直線で結ぶように指示する。指示は，"Draw a line between 92 and 100." や "Draw another one from 100 to 40." のように出す。
2. 活動を終えたら生徒に自分のシートを教師に見えるように掲げさせる。教師は拡大コピーしたピクチャーグリッドを生徒に見せて，線が同じように引けたかどうか生徒に確認させる。
3. 生徒にペアを組ませ，それぞれのパートナーと背中合わせに椅子に座らせ，机を各自の前に置かせる。
4. 生徒全員に2枚のナンバーグリッドを配る。約5分間で点と点を結び2枚の絵を自由に描くよう指示する。きちんとした絵になっていなくても一向に構わない。生徒はパートナーの絵を見てはいけないし，隣の生徒の絵を真似してもいけない。2枚の絵がそれぞれできるだけ異なるものがよい。
5. さらに2枚のナンバーグリッドを生徒全員に配る。これらは相手の指示に従って書き込むためのものである。
6. 片方の生徒（Instruction Giver）は指示を出し，もう一方の生徒（Instruction Taker）はナンバーグリッドに指示どおりの直線を引いていく。Instruction Taker は，指示が理解できなかったときは相手に質問することができる。ただし，Instruction Giver は線の位置についてしか答えることができず，「家の絵」などのように絵の説明をしてはいけない。また，Instruction Taker が描き終えるまで互いに相手の絵を見てはいけない。Instruction Taker が絵を描き終えたら，互いに見せ合って確認する。
7. 役割を交替しながら，ナンバーグリッドがなくなるまで6の活動を繰り返す。

5. Dot to Dot

★ ★ ★

Students practice numbers by describing and drawing straight-line pictures.

Level:	Beginner
Purpose:	Speaking, Listening/Numbers
Materials:	Picture Grid (normal size and enlarged version), Five Number Grids for each student
Usage:	Practice, Review
Time:	*Preparation*—5 to 10 minutes *Activity*—30 to 50 minutes

● **Description of Activity** ●

1. Distribute a Number Grid (see p.24) to each student. Ensuring that none of them can see the Picture Grid (see p.25), have them reproduce it in pencil by telling them where to draw the lines: for example, "Draw a line between 92 and 100. Draw another one from 100 to 40...."

2. Have the students hold up their finished pictures and show them the enlarged version of yours. Students check their pictures.

3. Have students make pairs and sit back-to-back with their partners, with a desk in front of each of them.

4. Distribute two Number Grids to each student. Tell them to draw a different *straight-line* picture on each. The drawings don't have to be of recognizable objects: abstract designs are just as good, so students needn't worry if they aren't particularly artistic. They shouldn't let their partners see their pictures, and they shouldn't copy their neighbors' drawings. Encourage them to make each picture as different as possible. Allow five minutes or so for this.

5. Distribute a further two Number Grids to each student.

6. One student in each pair, the Instruction Giver, describes one of their pictures to their partner, the Instruction Taker, who reproduces it in pencil on one of the Grids. Instruction Takers can ask questions, but Instruction Givers can only specify the position of the lines—they must *not* describe their drawings in any other way, such as by saying, "It's a house." Neither student can look at the other's drawing until the Instruction Taker has finished: then they compare pictures.

7. The students swap roles, and repeat the procedure from step 6 until all four pictures have been described and drawn.

Number Grid

• 10	• 20	• 30	• 40	• 50	• 60	• 70	• 80	• 90	• 100
• 9	• 19	• 29	• 39	• 49	• 59	• 69	• 79	• 89	• 99
• 8	• 18	• 28	• 38	• 48	• 58	• 68	• 78	• 88	• 98
• 7	• 17	• 27	• 37	• 47	• 57	• 67	• 77	• 87	• 97
• 6	• 16	• 26	• 36	• 46	• 56	• 66	• 76	• 86	• 96
• 5	• 15	• 25	• 35	• 45	• 55	• 65	• 75	• 85	• 95
• 4	• 14	• 24	• 34	• 44	• 54	• 64	• 74	• 84	• 94
• 3	• 13	• 23	• 33	• 43	• 53	• 63	• 73	• 83	• 93
• 2	• 12	• 22	• 32	• 42	• 52	• 62	• 72	• 82	• 92
• 1	• 11	• 21	• 31	• 41	• 51	• 61	• 71	• 81	• 91

Picture Grid

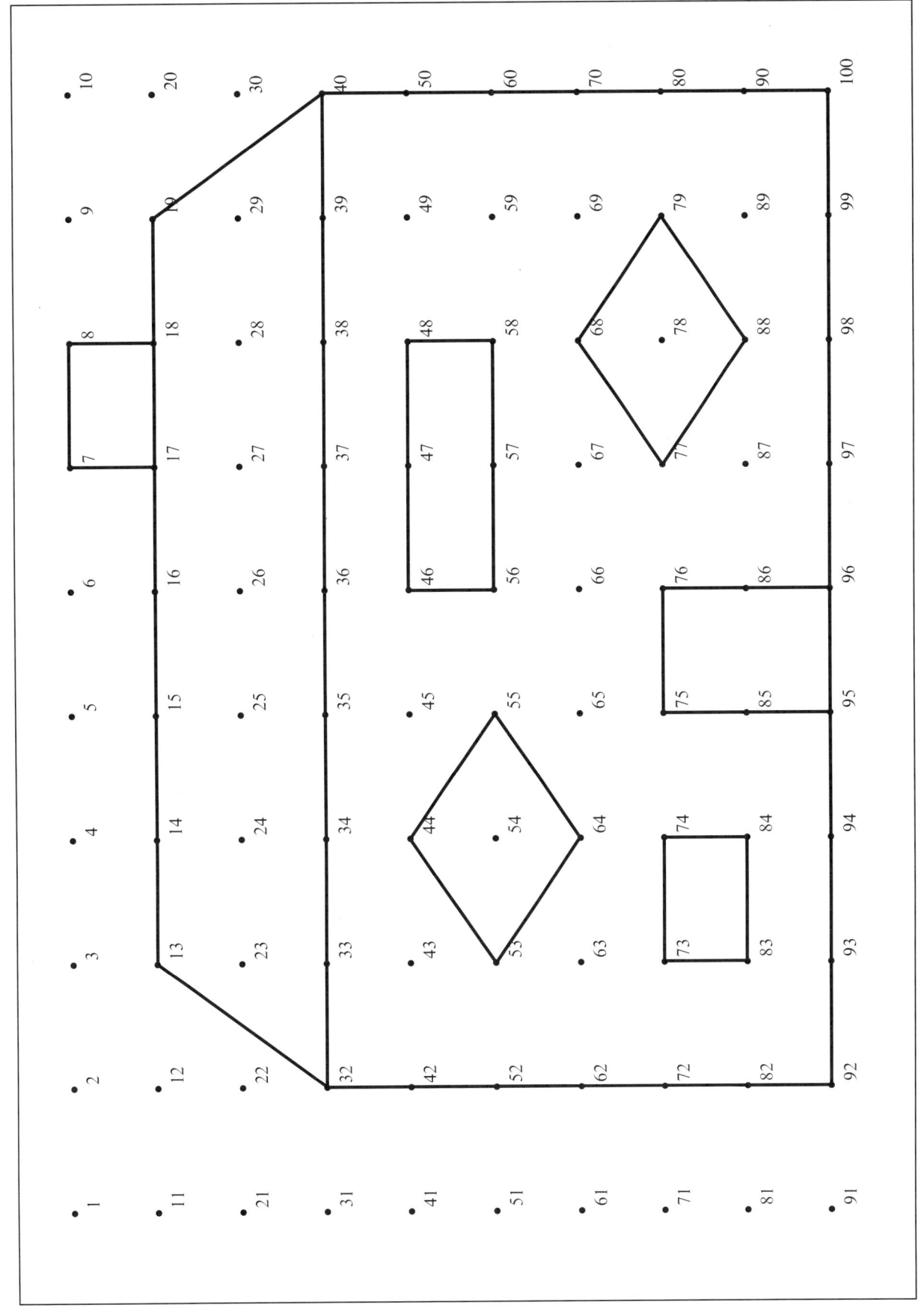

25

ACTIVITY 6 Which Hand Is the Dog In?

> ペアの1人が両手の中に1つずつ動物の絵カードを隠して持ち，相手に，ある動物がどちらの手に入っているか当てさせる活動。
>
> **Level:** 初級
> **Purpose:** Speaking／Vocabulary
> **Materials:** 動物の絵カード，ワークシート，はさみ
> **Usage:** 授業の中での活動，復習
> **Time:** 準備—5分　　活動—10～15分

● **Description of Activity** ●

1. 生徒に隣の席同士でペアを組ませ，机を移動してつけさせる。
2. 生徒全員に動物の絵カード(p.28参照)とワークシート(p.29参照)を配り，絵カードに描かれたそれぞれの絵の動物名を，教師の後について発音練習させる。
3. 動物の絵カードを，はさみで切り取らせる。
4. 活動について，実演しながら説明する。
   ①ペアの一方(A)は，両手の中に1つずつ動物の絵カードを持つ。相手(B)に何と何のカードを持っているかを言ってから，そのうちの1つがどちらの手に入っているかたずねる。
   ②BはAの片方の手を指しながら，左右どちらの手に入っているか言う。
   ③AはBが指した手を開き，答えが正しかったかどうか言う。正解ならば○を，違っていれば×を，各自のワークシートの表に記入する。
5. 活動開始。生徒は4の活動を1回したら役割を交替する。質問は交互に行い，全部で9回質問が終わったら活動を終了する。○の数が多いほうが勝ちとなる。

Model Dialogue (生徒の対話は次のようになる)
　A: I have a dog and a snake. Which hand is the dog in?
　B: It's in your right/left hand.
　A: That's right/wrong. [You're right/wrong.]

ひとことコーナー
・動物の名前の他に，果物，花，など色々な物の名前の定着を図ることができる。
・活動の回数は時間の都合で調整できる。

6. Which Hand Is the Dog In?

★   ★   ★

One student in a pair conceals two different animal picture cards, one in each hand. Their partner has to guess which animal is held in which hand.

Level: Beginner
Purpose: Speaking/Vocabulary
Materials: Sheet of animal cards for each student, Worksheet, Scissors
Usage: Practice, Review
Time: *Preparation*—5 minutes   *Activity*—10 to 15 minutes

● Description of Activity ●

1. Have the students make pairs with one of their neighbors. Have each pair move their desks and sit together.
2. Distribute a sheet of animal cards (see p.28) and a worksheet (see p.29) to each student. Say the names of the animals, and have the students repeat them.
3. Have the students cut out the pictures with scissors.
4. Demonstrate the activity.
   ①One student, A, in each pair has one animal card in each hand. A tells their partner, B, the names of the two animals they are concealing. A asks B to guess which hand one of the animals is in. See the Model Dialogue (p.26).
   ②B points to one of A's hands and says that the animal is in it.
   ③A opens the indicated hand and says whether B is right or not. Then each of them marks on their worksheets whether or not B's guess was correct.
5. Start the activity. Once the procedure in step 4 has been completed, have the students change roles and repeat nine times. The student who gets most points wins.

Additional Information

- Instead of the names of animals, you can use the names of fruits, flowers, and so on.
- You can adjust the number of times that students carry out the procedure according to the time available.

Animal Cards

duck	snake	tiger	lion
dog	giraffe	panda	turtle
rabbit	goat	cow	horse
cat	hippopotamus	crocodile	lizard
snail	crow	pigeon	butterfly

Worksheet

Which Hand Is the Dog In ?

Class _____   Name _____

対話例

A: I have a dog and a snake. Which hand is the dog in ?

B: It's in your right/left hand.

A: That's right/wrong. [You're right/wrong.]

Name	1	2	3	4	5	Total

Which Hand Is the Dog In ?

Class _____   Name _____

対話例

A: I have a dog and a snake. Which hand is the dog in ?

B: It's in your right/left hand.

A: That's right/wrong. [You're right/wrong.]

Name	1	2	3	4	5	Total

ACTIVITY 7

Find the Missing Letter

どこかつづりがおかしい単語を読み上げ，不足している文字や余分な文字を生徒に見つけさせる活動。

Level: 初級〜中級
Purpose: Listening/Spelling
Materials: なし
Usage: 復習
Time: 準備―10分　　活動―10〜20分

● Description of Activity ●

1. ある既習の単語を発音し，その単語の間違ったつづりを読み上げる。例えば，"Vacation. V-a-c-a-t-o-n." のように出題する。
2. 生徒は注意深く聞き，不足している文字(この場合は "i")を指摘する。その場で大きな声で答えさせてもよいし，挙手をして答えさせてもよい。
3. 正解した生徒には得点を与える。
4. 1〜3を繰り返し，一定時間内に最も多く得点した生徒が勝ちとなる。

▶**NOTE** 教師の読み上げるつづりを書き取ってもよいことにすれば，生徒は答えを見つけやすくなる。

ひとことコーナー

- 列ごとに得点を競わせることもできる。
- "Vacation. V-a-c-a-i-t-i-o-n." のように，余分な文字を指摘させる活動にすることもできる。
- 1つの課が終了してから行うなど，ある程度広い範囲から出題するほうが活動がおもしろくなる。

7. Find the Missing Letter

★　　　★　　　★

Students try to find missing or extra letters in words misspelt aloud by the teacher.

Level:	Beginner to Intermediate
Purpose:	Listening/Spelling
Materials:	None
Usage:	Review
Time:	*Preparation*—10 minutes *Activity*—10 to 20 minutes

● Description of Activity ●

1. Say an English word that students have already learned and then misspell it aloud. For example: "Vacation. V-a-c-a-t-o-n."
2. As soon as a student has spotted the mistake (the missing "i" in this example), they bring it to the teacher's attention, either by raising a hand or just calling out.
3. Award points to the student who answers correctly.
4. Repeat steps 1 to 3 with new words. The student who gets the most points during the time limit wins.

▶**NOTE** This activity will be easier for students if they can write the letters down as they are read out.

Additional Information

- If each row of students makes a team, competition between rows is possible.
- Have students find extra letters in words, for example, "Vacation. V-a-c-a-i-t-i-o-n."
- By using this activity at the end of a lesson, there will be more vocabulary items to choose from, making it more challenging.

ACTIVITY 8

How Do I Look?

ペアの一方が，顔や身体を使ってある感情を表現をする。もう一方はそれを見て，相手がどのように感じているのかを当てる活動。

Level: 初級〜中級
Purpose: Speaking, Listening／感情表現
Materials: ワークシート
Usage: ウォームアップ，授業の中での活動，復習
Time: 準備—5分　活動—10分

● Description of Activity ●

1. 生徒は自由に教室内を歩き回り，各自パートナーを見つける。
2. 生徒の一方(A)は顔や身体を使って自分の感情を相手(B)に伝え，"How do I look?"と尋ねる。
3. Bは，例えば"You look sad."と答える。Bは3回まで答えることができる。Bの答えが正解の場合，BはAのワークシートにサインする(p.34, Worksheet参照)。3回とも正解でない場合は×を記入する。
4. 生徒は役割を交替し，別の形容詞を使って2，3の活動を繰り返す。
5. 生徒は再び教室内を歩き回り，新しいパートナーを見つける。自分がそれまで使っていない形容詞を用いて，時間が許す限り活動を続ける。

▶NOTE　あらかじめ活動前に，感情を表す形容詞を復習したり，紹介しておくとよい。
　　　　例：cold, hot, great, happy, sad, sick, tired, angry, afraid, hungry, thirsty, sleepy, excited, nervous, bored, exhausted, irritated, etc.

ひとことコーナー

- 説明の際に教師がオーバーな表現を見せておくと，生徒も豊かな表情を作り楽しい雰囲気で進められる。
- 学級の雰囲気によっては男女のペアが作りにくいこともあるが，ワークシートのサイン欄を男女2つに分けておけば，自然と男女ペアを作らせることができる。異性からサインをもらった場合には得点をプラスするなどの工夫もできる。

8. How Do I Look?

★　　　★　　　★

> Students show their feelings to their partners through facial expressions and body language. Their partners have to guess how they feel.

Level: Beginner to Intermediate
Purpose: Speaking, Listening / Facial expressions
Materials: Worksheet
Usage: Warm-up, Practice, Review
Time: *Preparation*—5 minutes　　*Activity*—10 minutes

● Description of Activity ●

1. Students walk around the class and find a partner.
2. One of the students, A, makes a facial expression or uses body language to show their feelings and asks, "How do I look?"
3. Their partner, B, responds; for example, "You look sad." B is allowed up to three guesses. If B's guess is correct, then B signs A's worksheet (see p.34). If all three of B's guesses are incorrect, B signs and enters a cross onto A's worksheet.
4. The two students change roles and repeat steps 2 and 3 using a different adjective.
5. The students walk around the class again and find new partners. They cannot have the same partner more than once. They must use a different adjective with each partner. The activity continues until half the class have completed their worksheets.

▶**NOTE**　Before the activity begins, some suitable adjectives should be reviewed or introduced. For example: cold, hot, great, happy, sad, sick, tired, angry, afraid, hungry, thirsty, sleepy, excited, nervous, bored, exhausted, irritated, etc.

Additional Information

- In demonstrating the activity to the students, overact. Show the students how they can use their whole body to express their feelings, not just their face. This will create a good atmosphere.
- On the worksheet, there are two areas where students can sign. One is for girls' signatures, the other is for boys'. If students collect signatures of the opposite sex, award bonus points.

How Do I Look ?

Class _____ Name _____

男子からのサインはBoysの欄に，女子からのサインはGirlsの欄に記入してもらいましょう。異性からのサインは倍の得点になります。

	Signature		Wrong !
	Boys	**Girls**	
1			
2			
3			
4			
5			
6			
7			
8			
9			
10			
11			
12			

MEMO

ACTIVITY 9

Let's Play Cards!

カルタ取りの要領で，読み上げられたヒントに合う単語カードを取る活動。グループのなかで一番たくさんカードを取った人の勝ち。

Level: 初級〜中級
Purpose: Listening／Vocabulary
Materials: 単語カードシート（各グループに1枚ずつ），はさみ
Usage: 復習，定期試験後の授業等での投げ込み教材として
Time: 準備―5分　活動―15〜20分

● Description of Activity ●

1. クラスを4〜5人ずつのグループに分け，机を移動してグループごとにつけさせる。
2. 各グループに単語カードシート（p.38参照）を配る。カードをはさみで切り取らせ，机の上に表向きにばらまかせる。
3. 教師は単語のヒント（p.39, Word Hints参照）を読み上げ，生徒はそれにふさわしい単語カードを探す。最も多くカードを取った生徒が勝ちとなる。

ひとことコーナー

- 絵が得意な生徒に頼んでイラストのついたカードを作れば，それらの絵を見ながら生徒は喜んで活動する。
- ヒントを生徒に書かせると，ユーモアたっぷりのものが出てくる。

9. Let's Play Cards!

★   ★   ★

Students try to find word cards that match hints read out by the teacher. The student who collects the most cards wins.

Level: Beginner to Intermediate
Purpose: Listening/Vocabulary
Materials: Sheet of word cards for each group, Scissors
Usage: Review, Deviation from the textbook after an exam or a series of lessons
Time: *Preparation*—5 minutes   *Activity*—15 to 20 minutes

● **Description of Activity** ●

1. Divide the class into groups of four or five students. Have each group move their desks and sit together.
2. Give a sheet of word cards (see p.38) to each group. Have the students cut out the words. These are spread out on the desks, face up, so the students can see the words.
3. Read a word hint aloud (see p.39). Each student tries to be first to take the appropriate word card. The student with the most cards is the winner.

Additional Information

- Ask students who are good at drawing to make picture cards. Using these, students will be more willing to participate.
- If you let students write the hints, they often make up very humorous ones.

Word Cards

begin	fly	forget	lend	play
read	sing	tell	visit	wash
eyes	ears	hair	neck	foot
home	kitchen	chair	glass	breakfast
homework	station	hospital	village	hill
school	clouds	money	we	friend
student	hour	noon	weekend	yesterday
spring	ninety	twenty-nine	sixty-four	fifty-five
zero	English	Spanish	blue	black
white	few	poor	popular	same

9. Let's Play Cards!

Word Hints

Word	Hint
☐ begin	This means start.
☐ fly	Planes do this.
☐ forget	Not to remember
☐ lend	The opposite of borrow
☐ play	To enjoy yourself with your friends
☐ read	You do this with books.
☐ sing	You do this in *karaoke*.
☐ tell	To say something to someone
☐ visit	To go to see someone
☐ wash	To clean your body
☐ eyes	You have two of these on your face and you see with them.
☐ ears	You have two of these on your head and you hear with them.
☐ hair	This is on your head.
☐ neck	Above your shoulders, below your head
☐ foot	This is at the end of your leg.
☐ home	You live here.
☐ kitchen	You cook here.
☐ chair	You sit on this.
☐ glass	You drink from this.
☐ breakfast	You eat this in the morning.
☐ homework	Students do this at home for their teachers.
☐ station	People get on and off trains here.
☐ hospital	Sick people stay here.
☐ village	Smaller than a town
☐ hill	Lower than a mountain
☐ school	You learn here.
☐ clouds	These are white things in the sky.
☐ money	You buy things with this.
☐ we	You and me
☐ friend	Someone you like
☐ student	This is someone who studies at school.
☐ hour	60 minutes
☐ noon	12 o'clock
☐ weekend	Saturday and Sunday
☐ yesterday	The day before today
☐ spring	This is the season after winter.
☐ ninety	50 plus 40
☐ twenty-nine	15 plus 14
☐ sixty-four	50 plus 14
☐ fifty-five	15 plus 40
☐ zero	Nothing
☐ English	This is the language you are learning now.
☐ Spanish	People in Mexico speak this language.
☐ blue	The color of the sea and the sky
☐ black	The color of night
☐ white	The color of snow
☐ few	Not many
☐ poor	To have very little money
☐ popular	Liked by many people
☐ same	Not different

ACTIVITY 10

Who Am I ?

自分の背中に貼られたカードに書かれている人物は誰か，周りの人に質問しながら推測していく活動。

Level: 初級～上級
Purpose: Speaking
Materials: 人物名カード(生徒数分)，セロハンテープ
Usage: 定期試験後の授業等での投げ込み教材として
Time: 準備—5分　活動—20～30分

● Description of Activity ●

1. 授業の前に，誰もが知っている人物やキャラクターの名前が書かれたカード(p.42またはp.43，Name Cards 参照)を生徒数分用意しておく。
2. 人物名カードを裏向きにして，生徒全員に1枚ずつ配る。
3. 生徒は配られたカードをセロハンテープで隣の人の背中に留める。この時，相手にカードの名前を見られないように注意させる。
4. 生徒は教室の中を歩き回りながら相手を見つけて yes/no で答えられる質問をし，自分の背中の人物やキャラクターが誰なのか推測する。ただし，質問は1人に対して1回しかできないものとする(Sample Q&A 参照)。
5. 自分が誰か推測できたら，教師に知らせに行く。

▶NOTE　あらかじめ，生徒の間でよく知られている人物やキャラクターについて，情報を収集しておくとよい。
　　　　カードに書く人物やキャラクターの名前は日本語・英語のどちらでもよい。生徒のレベルやTTかどうかによって決めるとよい。

Sample Q&A
Name Card: Tiger Woods

A: Am I a man?　　　　　　　　　　　*B:* Yes.
A: Am I a professional sports player?　*C:* Yes.
A: Do I live in Japan?　　　　　　　　*D:* No.
A: Do I live in America?　　　　　　　*E:* Yes.
A: Do I play golf?　　　　　　　　　　*F:* Yes.
A: Am I Tiger Woods?　　　　　　　　*G:* Yes, that's right.

ひとことコーナー
- 日頃から生徒に身近な単語や興味・関心のある単語をたくさん与え，生徒のボキャブラリーを増やしておくことが活動を成功に導くコツである。
- ボキャブラリーがあまり豊かでないレベルの生徒には，人物やキャラクターの代わりにフルーツ，野菜，スポーツ，動物の名前などを用いて活動を進めると比較的スムーズにいく。

10. Who Am I?

★   ★   ★

Students ask each other questions to guess the names of the people that have been stuck on their backs.

Level: Beginner to Advanced
Purpose: Speaking
Materials: Name card for each student, Sticking tape
Usage: Deviation from the textbook after an exam or a series of lessons
Time: *Preparation*—5 minutes   *Activity*—20 to 30 minutes

● **Description of Activity** ●

1. Before class, cut out a different name card for each student (see Name Cards, p. 42 or p. 43).
2. In class, distribute one name card, face down, to each student.
3. Using sticking tape, each student attaches the card they were given to their neighbor's back. *Students must not know the names they have on their own backs.*
4. Students walk around the class and by asking yes/no questions, try to guess who they are. Students can only ask each of their classmates one question before moving on. See Sample Q&A (p. 40).
5. When they correctly work out their identity, they inform the teacher.

▶ **NOTE**   Before using this activity, try to get information from the students themselves about the people and characters who are well known to them.
   Choose either the Japanese or English name cards, according to the students' levels and whether or not the class will be team taught.

Additional Information

- Pre-teach any new vocabulary which the students will need to know in the lessons leading up to the one in which this activity will be used. Otherwise, it is likely that many of the identities will be guessed too easily.
- For students with a more limited vocabulary, this activity can be undertaken more successfully using the names of fruits, sports, animals and so on.

Name Cards (日本語版)

リンカーン	ジョン・F・ケネディ	ジョージ・ブッシュ
ヒラリー・クリントン	ダイアナ妃	エリザベス女王
ナイチンゲール	トーマス・エジソン	シェークスピア
モーツァルト	徳川家康	清少納言
夏目漱石	向井千秋	若田光一
タイガー・ウッズ	中田英寿	イチロー
松坂大輔	長嶋監督	貴乃花
武蔵丸	高橋尚子	田村亮子
ジョン・レノン	スティーブン・スピルバーグ	ブラッド・ピット
ミスター・ビーン	スーパーマン	KONISHIKI
木村拓哉	織田裕二	広末涼子
藤原紀香	浜崎あゆみ	宇多田ヒカル
倉木麻衣	GLAY	サンタクロース
シャーロック・ホームズ	シンデレラ	白雪姫
不思議の国のアリス	ハンプティ・ダンプティ	ミッキーマウス
くまのプーさん	スヌーピー	パディントン・ベア
ドラえもん	サザエさん	ピカチュー
キティちゃん	ゴジラ	ドラキュラ
(ALT の名前)	(校長先生の名前)	(クラスの生徒の名前)

(英語版)

Lincoln	John F. Kennedy	George Bush
Hillary Clinton	Princess Diana	Queen Elizabeth
Florence Nightingale	Thomas Edison	Shakespeare
Mozart	Tokugawa Ieyasu	Seishonagon
Natsume Soseki	Mukai Chiaki	Wakata Koichi
Tiger Woods	Nakata Hidetoshi	Ichiro
Matsuzaka Daisuke	Nagashima Kantoku	Takanohana
Musashimaru	Takahashi Naoko	Tamura Ryoko
John Lennon	Steven Spielberg	Brad Pitt
Mr. Bean	Superman	Konishiki
Kimura Takuya	Oda Yuji	Hirosue Ryoko
Fujiwara Norika	Hamasaki Ayumi	Utada Hikaru
Kuraki Mai	GLAY	Santa Claus
Sherlock Holmes	Cinderella	Snow White
Alice-in-Wonderland	Humpty Dumpty	Mickey Mouse
Winnie-the-Pooh	Snoopy	Paddington Bear
Doraemon	Sazae-san	Pikachu
Kitty-chan	Godzilla	Dracula
(ALT's Name)	(School Principal)	(Student in class)

ACTIVITY 11

Name the Animal

相手が思い浮かべた動物の名前を当てるゲームを通して，比較級を使った文に慣れる活動。

Level: 初級～中級
Purpose: Speaking, Listening／比較級の定着
Materials: ワークシート
Usage: 授業の中での活動，復習
Time: 準備―5分　活動―10～30分

● Description of Activity ●

1. 生徒全員にワークシート(pp.46-47参照)を配り，形容詞リストと動物リストに表記されている単語の発音と意味を確認する。
2. 生徒にペアを組ませ，各自に，動物リストに描かれている絵の中から好きな動物を1つ選んで心に思い浮かばせる。
3. ペアの1人が質問をして，相手が思い浮かべた動物を当てていく。質問を受けた生徒は，必ず比較級の文を使って答える(Sample Dialogue 参照)。
4. 答えが当たったら役割を交替する。
5. それぞれが3ラウンド質問をしたら終了する。

Sample Dialogue

A: What animal am I thinking of?
B: Is it a turtle?
A: No. It's faster than a turtle.
B: Is it a mouse?
A: No. It's more dangerous than a mouse.
B: Is it a tiger?
A: No. It's longer than a tiger.
B: Is it a crocodile?
A: Yes, it is.

ひとことコーナー

・動物名の他に果物，スポーツ，国の名前などでも活動ができる。
・この活動はグループで行うこともできる。
・生徒はゲーム感覚でたくさんの単語を覚えることができ，同時に比較級の文の定着も図れる。

11. Name the Animal

★   ★   ★

Using comparative sentences, students guess the names of animals.

Level: Beginner to Intermediate
Purpose: Speaking, Listening/Comparative expressions
Materials: Worksheet
Usage: Practice, Review
Time: *Preparation*—5 minutes   *Activity*—10 to 30 minutes

● Description of Activity ●

1. Give a worksheet (see pp. 46-47) to each student. Make sure the pronunciation and meaning of the words on the adjective list and the animal list are understood.
2. Have the students make pairs. Each student thinks of an animal from the animal list without telling their partner what it is.
3. One student in each pair tries to guess what animal their partner has in mind by asking questions. Their partner answers using a comparative sentence (see the Sample Dialogue, p. 44).
4. Once the animal has been identified, the students change roles and repeat step 3. This completes the first round.
5. Have the students play three rounds in all.

Additional Information
- Besides animals, this activity can also be carried out with fruits, sports, countries and so on.
- This activity can be undertaken in groups as well as in pairs.
- Students can build their vocabulary as well as practice the comparative while enjoying this activity.

Adjective List（形容詞リスト）

cute	ugly
big	small
tall / long	short
quiet	loud / noisy
exciting	boring
fat	thin
wild	tame
faithful	cunning
strong	weak
fast	slow
friendly	dangerous
heavy	light
large	small
fearless / brave / courageous	timid / cowardly
hairy	hairless

※上のリストになくても，知っている形容詞があれば積極的に使ってみましょう。

Animal List (動物リスト)

duck	snake	tiger	lion
dog	giraffe	panda	turtle
rabbit	goat	cow	horse
cat	hippopotamus	crocodile	lizard
snail	crow	pigeon	butterfly

ACTIVITY 12

Q&A Maze Game

すごろく形式のゲームをしながら，日常生活で使われるやさしい表現の定着を図る活動。

Level: 初級～中級
Purpose: Listening, Speaking, Writing
Materials: ワークシート，サイコロ，マグネットを貼った Maze Sheet，コマ用のマグネットを4つ
Usage: 授業の中での活動，復習
Time: 準備―15分　　活動―30～50分

● Description of Activity ●

1. TT の授業で，クラスを2つに分け，さらにそれぞれをAとBの2チームに分ける。
2. 模造紙大に拡大した Maze Sheet (p.50参照)を黒板に2枚貼り，それぞれの Maze Sheet に2つのマグネットをチームのコマとしてスタート地点に置く。
3. 初めにAチームの最初の生徒がサイコロを振り，出た目の数だけコマを進める。教師はコマが止まった地点の数字と同じ番号の質問を出題する(p.51参照)。正解したらコマをその地点に留めておくことができるが，間違えたらもとの位置に戻さなければならない。
4. 次にBチームの最初の生徒が3の活動をする。再びAチームの2番目の生徒が行い，Bチームの2番目の生徒が続く，という順序で進めていく。
5. 最初にゴールしたチームが勝ちとなる。ただし，ゴールする時は数が余らないようにしなければならない(例えば，ゴールするのに4が出ればいいときに5が出た場合は，マグネットを動かしてはいけない)。
6. 勝敗が決まったところでワークシート(p.51参照)を配り，生徒に答えを記入させる。

▶NOTE　Maze Sheet のはしごのついた番号に止まったときは，質問に正しく答えられたらはしごを登れるが，間違えたら元の場所にもどる。また，矢印のついた番号に止まったときは，質問に正しく答えられたらその番号に止まれるが，間違えたら矢印の指す番号までもどる。
　　　　活動中は質問を聞くことに集中させるため，机上に何も出させないようにするとよい。

ひとことコーナー

- ワークシートに記入させる時間がない場合は，宿題にしてもよい。
- TT のクラスで行うことにしたのは，クラスを4チームに分けるためである。日本人教師単独の授業では2チームにしか分けられず，40人近いクラスでは生徒の活動への参加の度合が低くなるからである。

12. Q&A Maze Game

★　　★　　★

Using a board game format, students familiarize themselves with useful daily expressions.

Level: Beginner to Intermediate
Purpose: Listening, Speaking, Writing
Materials: Worksheet, Two dice, Two magnetized Maze Sheets, Four board magnets
Usage: Practice, Review
Time: *Preparation*—15 minutes   *Activity*—30 to 50 minutes

● Description of Activity ●

1. In a team-taught lesson, divide the class into two. Each half should in turn be divided into two teams, A and B.
2. Put two Maze Sheets (enlarged from p.50 on a copier, and with magnetic strips fixed to their backs) on the board, and have each team put its magnet at the starting point. (All members of a team share the same magnet.)
3. One of the students from team A throws the dice, then moves the team magnet the number of spaces indicated. Ask the question that corresponds to the location of the magnet (see p.51). If the student answers the question correctly, the magnet stays where it is. If the answer is incorrect, it is moved back to its previous position.
4. The first student from B follows the procedure in step 3. After this, the second student from A carries out the procedure, followed by the second student from B, and so on.
5. The team which reaches the goal first wins. The goal must be reached by an exact throw of the dice. (So if a "4" is required to reach it, and the student throws a "5," the magnet may not be moved.)
6. As soon as there is a winning team, distribute a worksheet (see p.51) to each of the students, and have them complete it.

▶**NOTE** When a student lands on the bottom of a ladder, they only ascend if they answer correctly; otherwise they move back to their previous position. When they land on the tail of an arrow, they only descend if they answer incorrectly.

During the activity, have the students concentrate on listening to the questions. Don't let the students have anything on their desks.

Additional Information

- If there is insufficient time in class for students to complete the worksheet (step 6), have them finish it for homework.
- This activity should be used in team-taught lessons since the class can then be divided into four teams. Only two teams would be possible in a JTE solo class, and so student participation would be less.

Maze Sheet

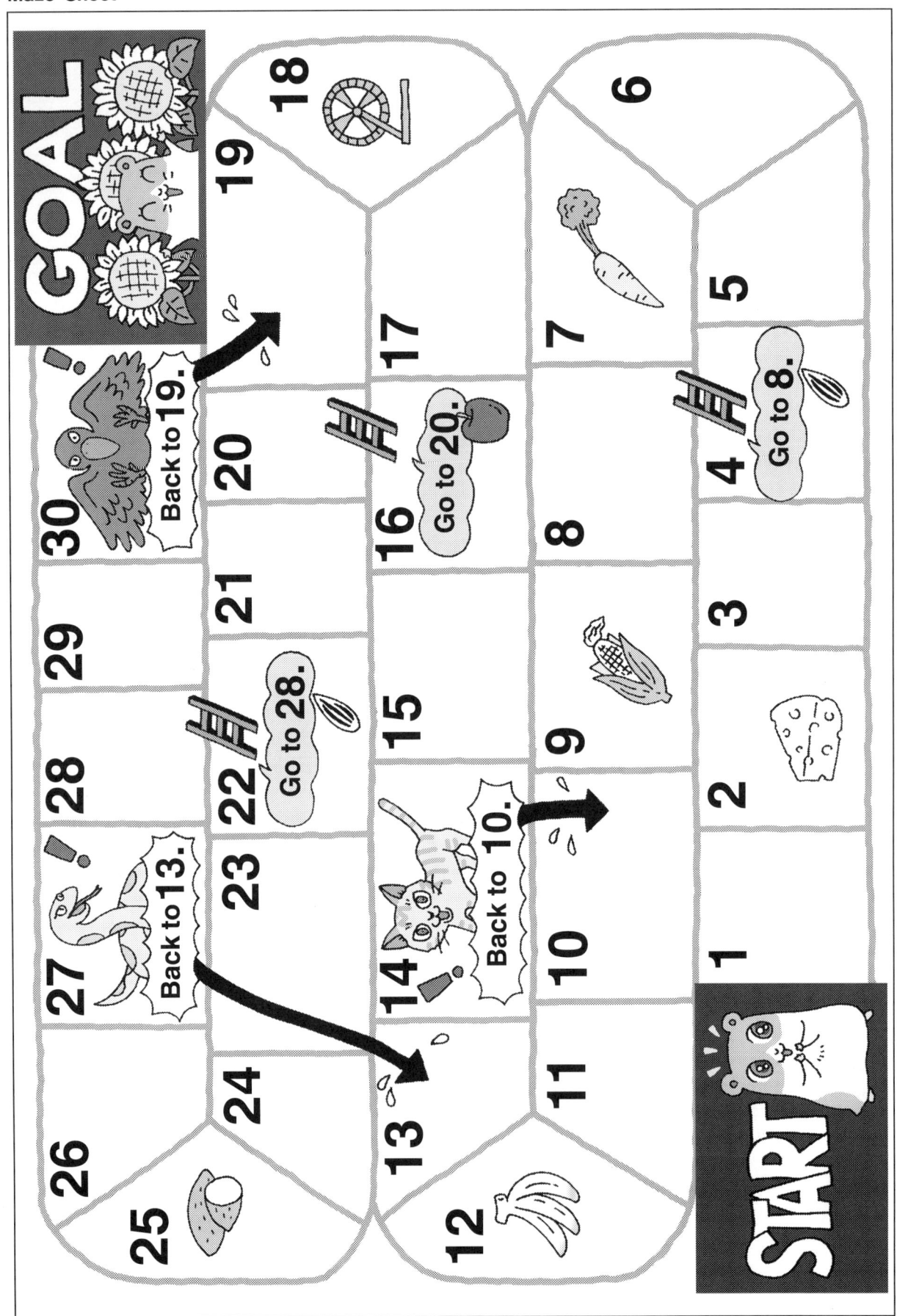

Q&A Maze Game

Class _____ Name _____

1. What time is it?
2. Are you American?
3. Aren't you American?
4. What's your name?
5. What's your homeroom teacher's name?
6. How old are you?
7. When's your birthday?
8. What day is it today?
9. Which do you like better, history or math?
10. Do you like basketball?
11. How's the weather today?
12. How was the weather yesterday?
13. Can you drive a car?
14. What's your favorite food?
15. How many brothers and sisters do you have?
16. What sports do you like?
17. How do you come to school?
18. Do you play the guitar?
19. What color do you like best?
20. What did you do on the weekend?
21. What will you do on the weekend?
22. Where do you live?
23. What time do you have lunch at school?
24. What time do you have lunch on Sundays?
25. How many students are there in this class?
26. How are you?
27. When do you usually get up?
28. What television program do you like best?
29. Have you ever been to Europe?
30. What do you have for breakfast?

ACTIVITY 13

Making Words

与えられた単語のつづり字をいくつか組み合わせて，別の単語をできるだけ多く作る活動。

Level: 初級～中級
Purpose: Vocabulary
Materials: アルファベットカード，メモ用紙(それぞれグループ数分)
Usage: ウォームアップ，定期試験後の授業等での投げ込み教材として
Time: 準備―10分　活動―10～15分

● Description of Activity ●

1. クラスを4人ずつのグループに分け，机を移動してグループごとにつけさせる。各グループにメモ用紙を1枚ずつ配る。
2. 生徒に活動について説明する(Example 参照)。
   ①アルファベットを1文字ずつ書いたカードを何枚か黒板に貼り，1つの単語を提示する。
   ②与えられた単語のつづり字をいくつか組み合わせて，別の単語を作って見せる。
3. 各グループに問題となる単語に必要なアルファベットカードを渡し，黒板にもカードを並べて問題の単語を提示する。一定の時間を与え，各グループにできるだけ多くの単語を作らせる。また，与えられた用紙に出来上がった単語をメモさせる。
4. 一定時間が過ぎたら終了し，各グループの代表は前に出て，出来上がった単語を黒板に書く。最も多く単語を作ったグループが勝ちとなる。
5. 3，4の活動を数回繰り返す。

▶NOTE　黒板に貼るアルファベットカードは，生徒によく見えるように大きめのものを使うようにする。

Example (作れる単語の例)

| S | T | A | P | L | E | R |

1文字……a
2文字……as, at
3文字……ate, ear, let, pet, rat, set, tea, etc.
4文字……ears, eats, late, let's, real, star, step, tape, tear, etc.
5文字……later, paste, plate, stare, tapes, etc.
6文字……plates, staple, etc.
7文字……plaster

Example Words to Give to Students (活動に使える単語の例)

AMERICAN	ANOTHER	ATMOSPHERE	BREAKFAST
BIRTHDAY	ESCALATOR	INTERNATIONAL	SHOULDER
REFRIGERATOR	INTERESTING		

13. Making Words

★　　★　　★

Students make words from the constituent letters of a given word.

Level:	Beginner to Intermediate
Purpose:	Vocabulary
Materials:	Letter cards, Sheet of blank paper for each group
Usage:	Warm-up, Deviation from the textbook after an exam or a series of lessons
Time:	*Preparation*—10 minutes　　*Activity*—10 to 15 minutes

● **Description of Activity** ●

1. Divide the class into groups of four students. Have each group move their desks and sit together. Give a sheet of paper to each group.

2. Demonstrate the activity. See Example, p.52.
　①Put some letter cards on the board to make a word.
　②Show some other words that can be made from this word.

3. Give each group the letter cards they will need to make a particular word. Then make this word on the board from letter cards. Allow the students a few minutes to write down as many words as they can make from the given word on their sheets of paper.

4. When time is up, a representative from each group should write their words on the board. The group with the most words wins this round.

5. Repeat steps 3 and 4 as often as desired.

▶**NOTE**　The letter cards used on the board should be large enough so that every student can see them clearly.

ACTIVITY 14

Rows and Columns

> 座席の縦と横の列の生徒が交互に起立し，教師の質問にスピーディーに答えていく活動。
>
> **Level:** 初級〜上級
> **Purpose:** Listening, Speaking
> **Materials:** 質問リスト
> **Usage:** ウォームアップ，復習
> **Time:** 準備―10分　　活動― 5 〜50分

● **Description of Activity** ●

1. 縦1列の生徒を起立させる。教師は質問をし(pp.56-61, 150 Questions 参照)，わかった生徒は挙手をする。最初に正解した生徒は席に座る。さらに質問を続け，正解した生徒は順次座っていく。最後にその列の1人が残る。
2. 今度は最後に残った生徒のいる横列が全員起立し，1を繰り返す。
3. このように，縦と横の列の生徒を交互に起立させながら，時間がくるまで活動を続けていく。

▶**NOTE** 同じ生徒が2回続けて最後の1人になった場合は，3回目の第1問はその生徒に優先的に答えるチャンスを与える。この時には必ず正解できる易しい質問にするように配慮したい。

ひとことコーナー

- 挙手をして指名されてから答えるのではなく，わかった瞬間に大きな声で答えるやり方もある。易しい質問の時は，このほうがスピーディーに活動を展開させられる。
- 質問はどんなものでもよい。What is this? のレベルから，Name a city in Spain beginning with B. のようにレベルを上げた質問へつなげるとよい。『言語活動成功事例集』pp.47-51 の「授業で使えるカテゴリー別 Question 150」も参照してほしい。
- 絵を見せて，そこに見たものを言わせたり(p.70, 16. What Do You See? 参照)，名詞の単数形を複数形に，動詞の原形を過去形に言い換えさせるなど，応用範囲の広い活動である。

14. Rows and Columns

★ ★ ★

Rows and columns of students stand up in turn to answer questions as quickly as possible.

Level: Beginner to Advanced
Purpose: Listening, Speaking
Materials: Question list
Usage: Warm-up, Review
Time: *Preparation*—10 minutes   *Activity*—5 to 50 minutes

● Description of Activity ●

1. Have one row of students stand. Ask them a question (see 150 Questions, pp. 56-61). If any of the standing students know the answer, they raise their hands. The first student to give the correct answer sits. Continue asking questions. Students who answer correctly sit. Finally one student will be left standing.
2. All the students sitting in the column of the standing student stand. The procedure in step 1 is repeated with this column.
3. Continue the activity having rows and columns of students stand in turn until time is up.

▶NOTE   If the same student is the last one standing on two occasions, then give them priority in answering the next question. Be sure to ask an easy one.

Additional Information

- Instead of raising their hands, students can call out the answers. If the questions are fairly simple, the activity will be faster.
- Any question type is acceptable. It is better to start with simple questions like "What is this?", and then make them progressively more difficult, for example, "Name a city in Spain beginning with B." Please see "Question 150" in *Communication Activities Book 1*, pp. 47-51 for further questions.
- You can also show a picture and have the students describe what they see (see Activity 16, What Do You See?, p. 70). This activity is also very suitable for having students give the plurals of nouns, change verbs into the past tense, and so on.

14. Rows and Columns

150 Questions

　問題は初めから順番に出すのではなく，生徒の学習レベルも考慮しつつ，同じ分野のものが続かないようランダムに出題する。一度出題した問題には□にチェック(✓)を付けるようにするとよい。ただし，□のない問題は，前の問題に続けて出題するようにする。

Letters of the alphabet

☐What letter is before P?　　　　　　　　　　　　—O
☐What letter is after J?　　　　　　　　　　　　　—K
☐What's the eighth letter of the alphabet?　　　　—H
☐What are the first five letters of the alphabet?　　—A, B, C, D, E
　What are the next five letters of the alphabet?　　—F, G, H, I, J
☐What are the last five letters of the alphabet?　　—V, W, X, Y, Z
☐Say the last three letters of the alphabet backwards.　—Z, Y, X
☐What is the last letter of the word "speak"?　　　—K
☐What is the first letter of the word "phone"?　　　—P
☐What is the third letter of the word "please"?　　—E

Numbers

☐What number is after 15 [16/17/18/19]?　　　　—16 [17/18/19/20]
☐What number is after 50 [60/70/80/90]?　　　　—51 [61/71/81/91]
☐What number is before 14 [15/16/17/18]?　　　—13 [14/15/16/17]
☐What number is before 40 [50/60/70/80]?　　　—39 [49/59/69/79]
☐What number is after 99?　　　　　　　　　　　—100
☐What number is between 59 and 61?　　　　　　—60
☐What's next?　60, 70, 80, 90, ＿＿＿.　　　　　　—100
☐What's next?　16, 17, 18, 19, ＿＿＿.　　　　　　—20
☐What's next?　11, 13, 15, 17, 19, ＿＿＿.　　　　—21
☐What's four plus seven?　　　　　　　　　　　　—Eleven
☐What's four times five?　　　　　　　　　　　　—Twenty
☐Say the numbers from one to six.　　　　　　　—1, 2, 3, 4, 5, 6
☐Say the numbers from six to ten backwards.　　—10, 9, 8, 7, 6
☐How many students are there in this room?　　—Open (39, 40, 41, etc.)
☐How many students [boys/girls] are standing?　—Open (Only me, 2, etc.)
☐How many students [boys/girls] are sitting?　　—Open (36, about 35, almost everyone, everyone else, etc.)
☐How many chairs are there in this room?　　　—Open (40, etc.)
☐How many pages are there in your English textbook?　—Open (128, etc.)
☐How many seasons are there in a year?　　　　—Four
☐How many players are there in a soccer team?　—11
☐How many letters are there in the alphabet?　　—26
☐How many days of the week end in y?　　　　　—Seven *or* All of them
☐How many brothers and sisters do you have?　—Open (None (*NOT* No-one/Nobody), one, etc.)

14. Rows and Columns

Words

- ☐ Spell "English." — E-N-G-L-I-S-H
- ☐ Spell "room." — R-O-O-M
- ☐ Say "on" backwards. — No
- ☐ Say "dog" backwards. — God
- ☐ Say "stop" backwards. — Pots
- ☐ Say "noon" backwards. — Noon
- ☐ Say "eye" backwards. — Eye
- ☐ Make a word from all these letters: H N G E I L S. — ENGLISH
  (*Write them on the board.*)
- ☐ Say one word starting with u. — Open (Uncle, under, understand, up, us, use, useful, usually, etc.)
- ☐ Say two words ending in l. — Open (All, April, beautiful, girl, pencil, school, well, etc.)
- ☐ Say two words beginning with w. — Open (Wait, walk, want, warm, wash, watch, water, wear, white, winter, work, world, write, etc.)
-   Say another two words beginning with w. — Open (*See previous answer.*)
- ☐ Say three words beginning with a. — Open (About, after, afternoon, again, all, always, animal, another, answer, ask, aunt, away, etc.)
-   Say another three words beginning with a. — Open (*See previous answer.*)
- ☐ Name three things in this room. — Open (Books, chairs, desks, lights, lockers, paper, pencils, etc.)
-   Name another three things in this room. — Open (*See previous answer.*)
- ☐ What is the name of the room where you cook? — Kitchen
- ☐ What is the name of the room where you eat? — Open (Dining room, canteen, kitchen, etc.)
- ☐ What is *jitensha* in English? — Bike *or* bicycle
- ☐ Say "*Eigo ga suki desu*" in English. — I like/love English.
- ☐ Make a sentence with the word "can't." — Open (I can't sing, I can't drive, etc.)
- ☐ Make a sentence with the word "teacher." — Open (You are a teacher, I'm not a teacher, etc.)

Time

- ☐ What time is it now? — Open (*9.10:* Nine ten *or* ten after/past nine, *9.30:* Nine thirty *or* half (past) nine, *10.07:* Ten (oh) seven *or* seven minutes after/past ten, *11.50:* Eleven fifty *or* ten before/of/till/to twelve, *12.00:* Twelve (o'clock) *or* midday *or* noon, *2.15:* Two fifteen *or* (a) quarter after/past two, *2.45:* Two

14. Rows and Columns

☐ What time do you eat breakfast?

☐ What time do you get up in the morning?
☐ What time will this lesson finish?
☐ What time will the next lesson start?

Days of the week
☐ What day is before Friday?
☐ What day is after Sunday?
☐ Say three days of the week.

Say another two days of the week.
Say the other two days of the week.
☐ Say the days of the week that begin with T.
☐ Say the days of the week that begin with S.

Months
☐ What is the second month of the year?
☐ What is the last month of the year?
☐ What is the month before September?
☐ What is the month after February?
☐ What is the month between May and July?
☐ Say the months beginning with J.
☐ Say the months ending in r.

☐ Which months begin with A?
☐ What is the coldest month in your town?
☐ Which month has the smallest number of letters?

Dates
☐ What's today's date?

☐ What was yesterday's date?

☐ What's tomorrow's date?
☐ When is your birthday? (*Note: If a student states their year of birth in their answer, this is incorrect.*)

☐ When does the next school vacation start?

—forty-five *or* (a) quarter before/of /till/to three, etc.)
—Open (*See previous answer for example permutations.*)
—Open (*See above.*)
—Open (*See above.*)
—Open (*See above.*)

—Thursday
—Monday
—Open (Monday, Tuesday, Wednesday, Thursday, Friday, Saturday, Sunday)

—Open (*See previous answer.*)
—Open (*See above.*)
—Tuesday, Thursday
—Saturday, Sunday

—February
—December
—August
—March
—June
—January, June, July
—October, September, November, December

—April, August
—Open
—May

—Open (June 4th (2002), Friday November 16th, etc.)
—Open (*See previous answer for example permutations.*)
—Open (*See above.*)
—Open (Today, next week, next Friday, next month, in (the) summer, November 16th, etc.)

—Open (Next week, next Tuesday, next month, (in) December, (on) December 23rd, etc.)

14. Rows and Columns

Seasons

☐ Name two seasons. —Open (Spring, summer, fall/autumn, winter)

  Name the other two seasons. —Open (*See previous answer.*)
☐ What is your favorite season? —Open (*See above.*)
☐ What season is it in Australia now? —Open (*Opposite to the season in Japan*)

Years (*When the present year is 2001*)
☐ What year is it now? —*2001*
☐ What year was it four years ago? —*1997*
☐ What year was it ten years ago? —*1991*
☐ What year was it 25 years ago? —*1976*
☐ What year was it a hundred years ago? —*1901*
☐ What year was it 350 years ago? —*1651*
☐ What year was it last year? —*2000*
☐ What year was it the year before last? —*1999*
☐ What year will it be next year? —*2002*
☐ What year will it be the year after next? —*2003*
☐ What year were you born? —Open

Weather

☐ What's the weather like today? —Open ((It's) Fine, sunny, cloudy, rainy, great, beautiful, bad, terrible, hot, cold, it's snowing, there's a typhoon, etc.)

☐ What was the weather like yesterday? —Open ((It was) Fine, cloudy, it snowed, there was a typhoon, etc.)

☐ What do you think the weather will be like tomorrow? —Open ((I think) (It'll be) Fine, cloudy, it'll snow/rain, there'll be a typhoon, etc.)

Colors
☐ Name a color beginning with p. —Open (Pink, purple, etc.)
☐ What color are kiwi fruit? —Green
☐ What color are tomatoes? —Red
☐ What color are your socks? —Open (White, black, blue, etc.)
☐ What's your favorite color? —Open (Green, yellow, red, etc.)
☐ Name two fruits which are red. —Open (Strawberries, apples, etc.)

Sports
☐ Name a sport beginning with b. —Open (Baseball, badminton, basketball, etc.)

  Name another sport beginning with b. —Open (*See previous answer.*)

14. Rows and Columns

☐What is your favorite sport? —Open (Judo, running, swimming, etc.)

Music (The Beatles)

☐Name one Beatles' song. —Open ("Help!", "Hey Jude", "Let It Be", "Yellow Submarine", etc.)

☐Sing a little of that song. —Open ("Let it be, Let it be, Let it be, Let it be, ...", etc.)

Geography

☐What is the capital of New Zealand? —Wellington
☐What is the capital of Great Britain? —London
☐What is the capital of Singapore? —Singapore
☐Beijing is the capital of what country? —China
☐What is the capital of South Korea? —Seoul
☐New Delhi is the capital of what country? —India
☐Name a famous city in the United States. —Open (Washington D.C., New York, San Francisco, etc.)

☐Is Alaska part of the United States? —Yes
☐Is Scotland part of England? —No
☐What is the longest river in Japan? —The Shinano
☐What is the highest mountain in Japan? —Mount Fuji
☐What is the largest ocean in the world? —The Pacific Ocean

Subjects

☐Name two subjects you study at school. —Open (Fine arts, domestic science, English, geography, history, Japanese, music, physical education, science, social studies, etc.)

Name another two subjects you study at school. —Open (*See previous answer.*)
☐What is your favorite subject at school? —Open (*See above.*)
☐What class is next? —Open (Japanese, history, this is the last class, etc.)

☐What class was before this one? —Open (Geography, music, this is the first class, etc.)

About students

☐What's your name? —Open
☐Can you play tennis? —Open (Yes, no, a little, etc.)
☐What's your hobby? —Open (Playing (the) guitar, collecting baseball cards, playing computer games, running, I don't have any hobbies, etc.)

14. Rows and Columns

☐What's your shoe size? —Open (23 cm, 24.5, large, small, about average, it's a secret, etc.)

☐What club do you belong to? —Open (Tennis club, soccer club, science club, art club, etc.)

☐Where do you live? —Open

☐How do you come to school? —Open (By bicycle, by train, on foot (*NOT by foot*), I walk to school (*NOT walking* OR *I come by walking*), etc.)

☐What do you do on the weekend? —Open (*Note: Students must answer using the present tense*—(I) Go out with my friends, play tennis, sleep, study, etc.)

☐What did you do on the weekend? —Open (*Note: Students must answer using the past tense*—(I) Went shopping, played tennis, etc.)

☐Have you ever been to another country? —Open (Yes, no, never, Malaysia, etc.)

☐What's the name of the person next to you? —Open

About the teacher

☐What's my name? —Open (Steven, Steven Ashton, Mr. Ashton, etc.)

☐What country am I / is our ALT from? —Open (Australia, Canada, Singapore, etc.)

☐Where do I live? —Open

☐What color is my hair? —Open (Black, blond(e), brown, etc.)

☐Who is taller, you or me? —Open (I am, me, you (are), etc.)

Showing something

☐Is this your book? (*Hold up a book.*) —Yes, no

☐What's this? (*Show an object to the students.*) —Open ((It's) A pencil, etc.)

☐What's this? (*Point to something, e.g. an article of clothing.*) —Open ((It's) A/Your shirt, etc.)

☐What's this? (*Point to a part of the body.*) —Open ((It's) Your arm, etc.)

☐What am I doing? (*Mime an action, e.g. running, jumping, opening a door, sleeping, opening a can of drink, taking a shower, etc.*) —Open ((You're) Running, jumping, etc.)

☐What does this gesture mean? (*Make a gesture.*) —Open (Come here, Good luck, Stop!, etc.)

61

ACTIVITY 15

Dash Off the Answer

早押しクイズ形式で，教師が出すクイズに正しく答えたチームが得点する。チーム同士で競いながら目標文を定着させる活動。

Level: 初級〜中級
Purpose: Listening, Writing／目標文の定着
Materials: Q&Aシート，解答シート(それぞれ生徒数分)，卓上ベル
Usage: 授業の中での活動，復習
Time: 準備—10分　　活動—25〜40分

● Description of Activity ●

1. 生徒全員に，解答シート(p.65参照)を1枚ずつ配布する。
2. クラスを列ごとに分け，それぞれチームを作る。
3. 教師は黒板に答えを書くスペースと得点表を作る(p.64参照)。
4. 生徒にルールを説明する。
　「これから質問をしますので，みなさんは答えを解答シートに書き込んでください。答えは必ず動詞を含んだ文の形にします。ただし，質問をした後すぐに，例えば"No.2"と番号を言います。そうしたら，前から2番目に座っている人は解答欄に答えを書く代わりに，前に出て黒板に答えを書きます。書き終わったら教卓のベルを押してください。正解で一番早くベルを押したチームに2ポイント，2番目のチームに1ポイント与えらえます。ただし，ベルを押した後で間違いに気づいても訂正はできません。」
5. 活動開始。p.66およびp.68の質問を使って4の活動を行い，得点を黒板の表に書き込む。
6. 活動終了後，参照用としてQ&Aシート(pp.66-67およびpp.68-69参照)を配布する。

▶**NOTE**　机の横にカバンなどを掛けておくと走り出す時に足を引っかけたりするので，あらかじめはずさせておく。
　　列の人数が少ない時や欠席の生徒がいる時は，すぐ前(または後ろ)の生徒が代わりに黒板に走るなどと決めておくとよい。

ひとことコーナー
- 縦の列のチームなので協力がしにくいように思えるが，実際には生徒は列で自然にかたまり，助け合って正解を探し，指名された番号の生徒を黒板へと走らせる。
- 共通のミスがはっきり出てくるので，要所要所で解説を入れると効果的である。
- 教師は質問をしたり得点を数えたりしなければならないので，TTの授業で実施するのがよい。

15. Dash Off the Answer

★　　　★　　　★

Teams compete in this quiz which tests students' knowledge of grammar and key expressions.

Level:	Beginner to Intermediate
Purpose:	Listening, Writing/Grammar, Key expressions
Materials:	Q&A sheet and answer sheet for each student, Bell
Usage:	Practice, Review
Time:	*Preparation*—10 minutes　　*Activity*—25 to 40 minutes

● Description of Activity ●

1. Distribute an answer sheet (see p.65) to each student.
2. Divide the class into as many teams as there are columns of students in front of the teacher.
3. Make an answer space for each team and a score sheet on the board. See p.64.
4. Demonstrate the activity.
   "I'm going to ask questions. Write down your answers on the answer sheets. *All answers must include a verb.* As soon as I have asked each question, I will say a number, for example, 2. All of the students sitting in that row must come to the board immediately and write the answer on the board, instead of on their answer sheets. Each student rings the bell as soon as they finish. The first student with the right answer to ring the bell gets two points for the team. The second student with the right answer to ring the bell gets one point. If you notice your answer is wrong after ringing the bell, you can't change it."
5. Start. Carry out the procedure described in step 4, keeping score, using one of the sets of questions on p.66 and p.68 until time is up. Announce the result.
6. After the activity is over, give the appropriate Q&A sheet (see pp.66-67 or pp.68-69) to each student to keep for reference.

▶**NOTE**　Don't let students hang their bags from the sides of their desks or in the gangways. As students dash for the board, such obstacles will present a tripping hazard.
　　　　Where a row for a given team lacks a student, then the student in the row in front acts in their place.

Additional Information

- Once the activity is underway, the teams of students will soon start to work together.
- Common mistakes will become apparent. Commenting on these as they occur will be very effective.
- Since the teacher has to read out the questions, comment on errors and keep score, this activity is best carried out in a team-taught lesson.

15. Dash Off the Answer

活動の形態

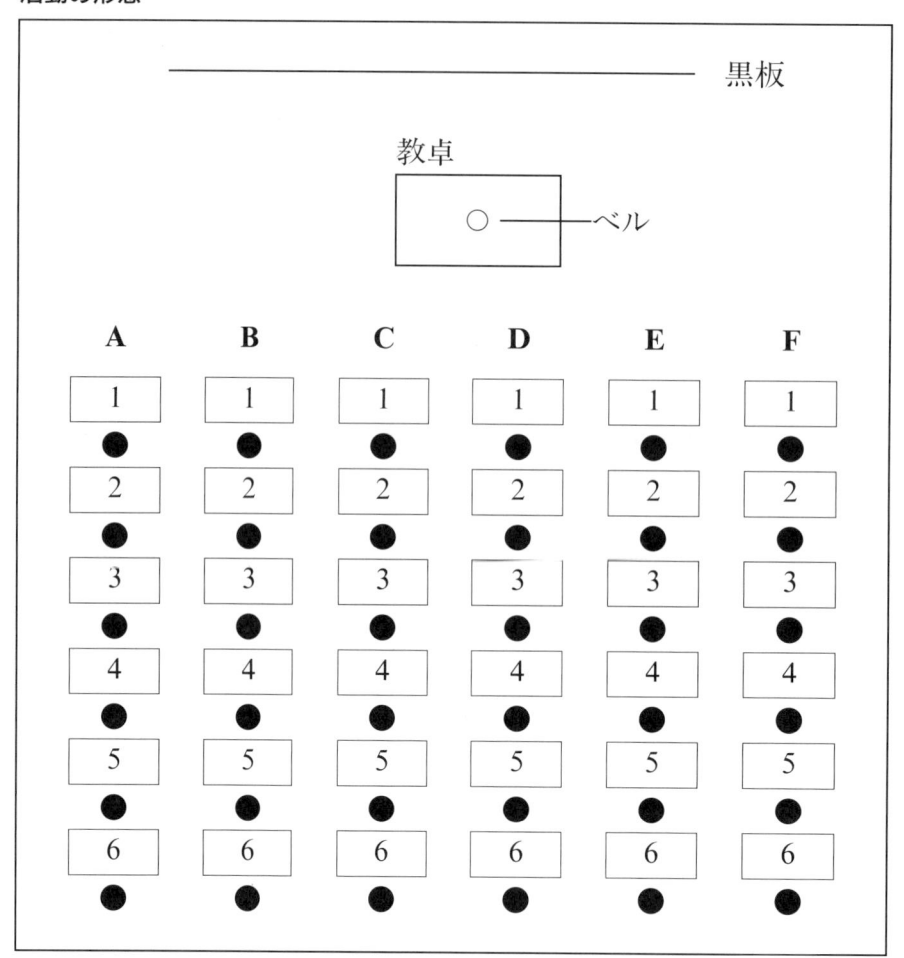

	黒板				

教卓 ○―ベル

A	B	C	D	E	F
1	1	1	1	1	1
●	●	●	●	●	●
2	2	2	2	2	2
●	●	●	●	●	●
3	3	3	3	3	3
●	●	●	●	●	●
4	4	4	4	4	4
●	●	●	●	●	●
5	5	5	5	5	5
●	●	●	●	●	●
6	6	6	6	6	6
●	●	●	●	●	●

黒板に設ける解答用スペース　　　　　　　　　　　　　　**得点表**

A	B	C	D	E	F

A	
B	
C	
D	
E	
F	

※男女で列が分かれる場合は2段にし，女子の列は下段に書くようにするとよい。

Answer Sheet

Dash Off the Answer

Class _____   Name _____

1. _____
2. _____
3. _____
4. _____
5. _____
6. _____
7. _____
8. _____
9. _____
10. _____
11. _____
12. _____
13. _____
14. _____
15. _____
16. _____
17. _____
18. _____
19. _____
20. _____
21. _____
22. _____
23. _____
24. _____
25. _____
26. _____
27. _____
28. _____
29. _____
30. _____

Q&A Sheet for the Introductory Level

Dash Off the Answer

Questions

1. Who are you?
2. How are you?
3. Are you a student?
4. Are you from Canada?
5. What time is it?
6. Can you speak French?
7. Do you like tennis?
8. Where do you live?
9. How do you come to school?
10. Are you hot?
11. When's your birthday?
12. When do you go to bed?
13. What subject did you study last night?
14. Do you play soccer?
15. Are you playing soccer now?
16. What fruit do you like best?
17. How many months are there in a year?
18. When do you clean your room?
19. Do you study English every day?
20. Did you go to the movies last week?
21. What are you doing now?
22. I have a brother. How about you?
23. Where's your bag?
24. I can play the guitar. How about you?
25. I like milk. How about you?
26. What do you do every weekend?
27. What did you do last weekend?
28. I have a small bag. How about you?
29. What time do you usually get up on Sundays?
30. Where did you go last Saturday?

Example Answers

1. I'm Erika./etc.
2. I'm fine./I'm okay./I'm so-so./I have a cold./I'm not so well./etc.
3. Yes, I am./etc.
4. No, I'm not./etc.
5. It's nine o'clock./etc.
6. Yes, I can./No, I can't./etc.
7. Yes, I do./No, I don't./etc.
8. I live in Fukuoka./etc.
9. I walk./I come by bicycle./etc.
10. Yes, I am./No, I'm not./etc.
11. It's on August 21st./etc.
12. I go to bed at eleven./etc.
13. I studied English./I didn't study./etc.
14. Yes, I do./No, I don't./etc.
15. No, I'm not.
16. I like apples best./etc.
17. There are twelve./etc.
18. I clean it on the weekend./I don't clean it./etc.
19. Yes, I do./No, I don't./etc.
20. Yes, I did./No, I didn't./etc.
21. I'm studying English./etc.
22. I have one, too./I have two brothers./I don't have any brothers./etc.
23. It's under the desk./It's in my room./etc.
24. I can, too./No, I can't./I can play a little./etc.
25. I like it, too./I don't like it./etc.
26. I play tennis with my friends./etc.
27. I played tennis with my friends./etc.
28. I have a small bag, too./I have a big bag./I don't have a bag./etc.
29. I get up at nine o'clock./etc.
30. I went to Harajuku./etc.

Dash Off the Answer

Questions
1. What time does school begin?
2. What do you usually do after school?
3. How many classes do you have tomorrow?
4. Did you watch television last night?
5. Were you at school last Friday?
6. Where were you yesterday evening?
7. What did you do yesterday evening?
8. What were you doing at seven o'clock this morning?
9. When will you get up tomorrow?
10. How's the weather today?
11. How was the weather yesterday?
12. How will the weather be tomorrow?
13. What are you going to do this weekend?
14. What do you think about baseball?
15. What time do you have to go to bed?
16. What do you want to do next summer?
17. Do you like taking pictures?
18. Which do you like better, spring or fall?
19. Have you ever visited Europe?
20. What did you eat for breakfast this morning?
21. What did you do after school yesterday?
22. Have you eaten your lunch yet?
23. How many times have you been to Australia?
24. When will you begin cleaning the school today?
25. How long have you been a student at this school?
26. When you got up this morning, what did you do?
27. How far is the station from here?
28. How was your weekend?
29. What will you do if it rains on the weekend?
30. How high can you jump?

Example Answers

1. It begins at eight thirty./etc.
2. I play baseball./etc.
3. I[We] have five./I[We] don't have any./etc.
4. Yes, I did./No, I didn't./etc.
5. Yes, I was./No, I wasn't./etc.
6. I was at home./etc.
7. I played a computer game./etc.
8. I was having breakfast./etc.
9. I'll get up at six thirty./I'll get up early./etc.
10. It's sunny[cloudy]./It's raining[snowing]./It's great./etc.
11. It was sunny[cloudy]./It rained[snowed]./It was great./etc.
12. (I think) It'll be sunny[cloudy]./It'll rain[snow]./It'll be great./etc.
13. I'm going to go shopping with my friends./I'm going to see a movie./etc.
14. I think it's great./I don't like it./etc.
15. I have to go to bed at ten o'clock./etc.
16. I want to have a vacation./etc.
17. Yes, I do./No, I don't./etc.
18. I like spring better./etc.
19. Yes, I have./No, I haven't.
20. I ate rice and soup./etc.
21. I went to drama club./etc.
22. Yes, I have./No, I haven't./etc.
23. I've been there once./I've never been there./etc.
24. We'll begin at three fifteen./etc.
25. I've been here for one year./I've been here since April this year./etc.
26. I ate breakfast./etc.
27. It's about 1 km from here./It's about 20 minutes by bus./etc.
28. It was a lot of fun./It was boring./etc.
29. I'll watch television./etc.
30. I can jump one meter./I don't know./etc.

ACTIVITY 16

What Do You See?

絵，写真やポスターのなかに見たものを，英語で発表する活動。

Level: 初級～中級
Purpose: Speaking, Listening
Materials: ポスター，雑誌，新聞，本などの絵や写真
Usage: ウォームアップ
Time: 準備―15分　活動―10～15分

● **Description of Activity** ●

1. 生徒全員を起立させ，大きめの絵かポスターを提示する。
2. 生徒に活動について説明する。
   ①生徒は挙手をして，絵やポスターのなかに見たものを英語で発表する。ただし，すでに他の生徒が発表した英文を繰り返すことはできない。
   ②発表した生徒は着席する。
3. 活動開始。クラスで半分以上の生徒が着席したら活動は終わりにする。

Example

I see a young lady.
Some boys are playing soccer.
There is a big tree near the soccer ground.

▶**NOTE** 活動に入る前に，表現の仕方について例を提示する。
既習の表現は何を用いてもよいこととする。また，少しでも長めの文で言うほうがよいと奨励する。例えば，I see a young lady. よりも I see a young lady wearing a hat. のほうが好ましい。
絵やポスターは，教室の一番後ろの生徒にも見える大きさのものを用意する。

🗨 ひとことコーナー
・提示する絵やポスターは，生徒が色についても表現できるようにカラーのものを選びたい。また，描写が細部にわたっているもののほうが，生徒のさまざまな表現を引き出すのに効果的である。

16. What Do You See?

★ ★ ★

Students take turns in describing a picture or poster in English.

Level: Beginner to Intermediate
Purpose: Speaking, Listening
Materials: Posters and pictures from magazines, newspapers and books
Usage: Warm-up
Time: *Preparation*—15 minutes   *Activity*—10 to 15 minutes

● Description of Activity ●

1. Have all the students stand. Show them a large picture or poster.
2. Demonstrate the activity to the students.
   ①Students raise their hands and speak about what they see in the picture or poster (see Example, p.70). They cannot repeat what other students have already said.
   ②After speaking, students sit down.
3. Start the activity. Continue until half the class are seated.

▶**NOTE**   Before beginning the activity, give an example.
   Students can use any of the expression types they have learned. Encourage the students to make sentences as long as possible. So, for example, "I see a young lady wearing a hat" is preferable to "I see a young lady."
   The pictures or posters should be large enough so that even the students at the back of the class can see clearly.

Additional Information
- Use color pictures so that students can describe the colors. Use detailed pictures so students can use a wide variety of expressions.

ACTIVITY 17

Concentration

決められた簡単な動作をグループで繰り返しながら，あるカテゴリーの語を一連の動作が終わる前に次々に言っていく活動。

Level: 初級～上級
Purpose: Speaking, Listening／Vocabulary
Materials: なし
Usage: ウォームアップ，定期試験後の授業等のでの投げ込み教材として
Time: 準備—なし　活動—10～20分

● Description of Activity ●

1. クラスを5，6人ずつのグループに分ける。机とイスを教室の後ろに移動して，各グループに円を作らせる。
2. 次の一連の動作を教え，全員そろってスムーズにできるようになるまで練習を繰り返す。
   ①両手をパンと1度たたく。
   ②両手を頭の上にのせる。
   ③両手で肩をたたく。
   ④両手で太ももをたたく。
3. 各グループにカテゴリーを1つ選ばせる(Example Categories 参照)。
4. グループで順番を決める。最初の生徒は，全員で2の動作を行っている間に自分のグループが選んだカテゴリーの語を1つ言う。例えば "Colors" を選んだ場合，"Blue" のように言う。次の生徒も2回目の動作の間に，"Green" などと続けていく。一連の動作の間に答えられなかった生徒は円から外れる。次に新しいカテゴリーを選んで同様に繰り返し，1人になるまで活動を続ける。
5. 最後に各グループの勝者が集まり，上記の活動を行ってクラスのチャンピオンを決める。

▶NOTE　あるカテゴリーでの活動の中では，一度言われた語を繰り返してはいけない。

Example Categories
- Letters of the alphabet
- Words ending with d
- Food or Drink
- Animals
- Numbers
- Good things
- Sports
- Parts of the body
- Words beginning with a or b
- Big things
- Colors
- Words with two or three letters

ひとことコーナー
・活動に入る前に，一連の動作を完全にマスターしておくことが大切である。

17. Concentration

★   ★   ★

While students repeat a cycle of very simple actions together in groups, they take it in turns to say words belonging to a certain category before a particular cycle is complete.

- **Level:** Beginner to Advanced
- **Purpose:** Speaking, Listening/Vocabulary
- **Materials:** None
- **Usage:** Warm-up, Deviation from the textbook after an exam or a series of lessons
- **Time:** *Preparation*—None   *Activity*—10 to 20 minutes

● Description of Activity ●

1. Divide the class into groups of five or six. Move the desks and chairs to the back of the room. Have each group make a circle.
2. Demonstrate the following series of actions and have the students repeat them until they can carry out the cycle smoothly:
   ①Clap your hands.
   ②Pat your head.
   ③Tap your shoulders.
   ④Pat your thighs.
3. Have each group choose a category. See Example Categories (p.72).
4. The students in each group decide their order—who will be first, second and so on. Then while all the students carry out one cycle of the actions described in step 2 simultaneously, the first student says a word belonging to the category—for example, "Blue" in the case of "Colors." The second cycle follows on from the first without interruption, and during this time the second student says something appropriate, such as "Green," and so on. When a student is unable to give an appropriate answer before the cycle is complete, they drop out of the circle. Then a new category is chosen and the other students continue in this way until there is just one remaining.
5. The winners from each group form a new group to decide the class champion.

▶**NOTE**   Once a word from a category has been said, it cannot be repeated.

Additional Information

- Before beginning the activity, ensure that students have mastered the cycle of actions.

ACTIVITY 18

Interviewing the ALT

あるグループが1つのトピックについてALTに質問し，ALTはそれに答える。次にJTEが他のグループに同じ質問をし，その質問に正しく答えられたグループが得点する活動。

Level: 初級～中級
Purpose: Listening, Speaking, Writing／異文化理解
Materials: B6判の用紙(生徒数分，さらに各グループに2枚ずつ)
Usage: 定期試験後の投げ込み教材として
Time: 準備―5～10分　活動―50分

● Description of Activity ●

1. クラスを4人ずつのグループに分け，机を移動してグループごとにつけさせる。
2. 生徒全員にB6判の用紙を1枚ずつ，さらに各グループに2枚ずつ配る。
3. まず，各グループはALTに質問するためのトピックを1つ決め(Sample Topics 参照)，グループに配られた2枚の用紙の上の部分に書く。次に，そのトピックについての質問を各自1問ずつ考え，自分の用紙に書く(Sample Questions 参照)。さらに，グループの2枚の用紙にも各自が考えた質問を書き，1枚はALTに提出し，もう1枚はグループでの参照用に持っている。
4. あるグループが前に出てきて，クラス全体に聞こえるようにALTに質問する。ALTはそれぞれの質問にわかりやすく答える。他のグループは答えをメモしておく。
5. 前に出たグループの質問がすべて終わったら，JTEは同じ質問を他のグループに向かってする。最も早く挙手して正解したグループに得点を与える。間違えた場合は減点となり，解答する権利は次に挙手したグループに移る。どのグループも答えられない場合は，もう一度担当グループがALTに質問し，正しく理解させる。
6. JTEの質問が終わったら次のグループが前に出て，4，5の活動を繰り返す。すべてのグループの質問が終わったら活動を終了し，最も多く得点したグループの勝ちとなる。

Sample Topics (All refer to life in the ALT's home country except *)
- Study at school
- School rules
- School clubs and teams
- The weekend
- Family Life
- Part-time jobs
- Vacations
- Customs
- Types of home
- Life in Japan*

Sample Questions (Part-time jobs の場合の例)
1. What part-time jobs do high school students do?
2. What was your part-time job?
3. How much money do you usually get an hour?
4. What did you do with the money?

18. Interviewing the ALT

▶**NOTE**　JTE は，生徒の質問が ALT に失礼にならないように注意させる。
　　　　　トピックと質問をあらかじめ提出させることで，生徒にわかりやすい答えを用意する時間を ALT に与えらえる。また，この質問用紙は JTE が他のグループに質問する際にも使う。

★　　　★　　　★

One group asks the ALT about a certain topic, and the ALT answers the questions. Then the JTE asks the same questions to the other groups in the class. The groups which answer correctly gain points.

Level:　　　Beginner to Intermediate
Purpose:　　Listening, Speaking, Writing／Understanding cultural differences
Materials:　Blank B6 sheet for each student, Two extra sheets for each group
Usage:　　　Deviation from the textbook after an exam or a series of lessons
Time:　　　*Preparation*—5 to 10 minutes　　*Activity*—50 minutes

● Description of Activity ●

1. Divide the class into groups of four students. Have each group move their desks and sit together.
2. Give each student a sheet of B6 paper and give each group two additional pieces of paper.
3. Each group selects a topic (see Sample Topics, p.74) and writes it at the head of both of the two sheets. Then each group member makes up one question on this topic on their sheet of paper (see Sample Questions, p.74). Also, group members write their questions on both of the two additional sheets. One of these is given to the ALT; the other is kept by the group for reference.
4. One group comes to the front of the class to ask its questions to the ALT in a loud voice. The ALT answers the questions very clearly. The other groups take notes.
5. When one group has finished, the JTE asks the same questions to the other groups in the class. Points are awarded to groups for correct answers, and are deducted for wrong ones (with the right to respond passing to another group). If no group can answer correctly, then the original group asks the ALT again, to ensure correct comprehension.
6. When the JTE has finished asking the questions, another group comes to the front of the class and steps 4 and 5 are repeated. Continue until all of the groups have finished. The group that gains the most points wins.

▶**NOTE**　The JTE should ensure that the groups' questions are not impolite.
　　　　　Having the groups submit their topics and questions in writing gives the ALT time to prepare answers in English of a suitable level. This sheet will also be used by the JTE when they ask the questions to the other groups.

ACTIVITY 19　Speaking Competition

学んだ表現を用いて各自1〜2文の英文を作り，クラスで発表する。他の生徒たちは発表を聞いて，内容がおもしろかった生徒と発表が上手かった生徒を投票で決めていく。

Level:　　初級〜中級
Purpose:　Speaking, Listening, Writing, Reading／目標文の定着
Materials:　投票用紙と清書用紙(それぞれ生徒数分)
Usage:　　授業中での活動，復習
Time:　　準備―5分　　発表―20〜30分

● Description of Activity ●

1. 生徒に学習した表現を用いてノートに1〜2文を作文させる(Example参照)。
2. 全員が書き終えた時点で，教師は投票用紙と清書用紙(p.78参照)を1枚ずつ配布する。
3. 発表のルールを説明する。
   ①挙手をして発表する。前の人が言った文と同じ文ではいけない。
   ②内容が一番おもしろかった生徒と発表が一番上手かった生徒を投票で選ぶので，ノートに必ずメモをとる。
4. 活動開始。挙手をした生徒から順次発表する。生徒は自分の発表が遅くなると，他の生徒が先に自分のと同じ文を発表してしまうのではないかと，先を争うように挙手をする。発表がよく聞こえない場合には，教師は "Please repeat that sentence." などと言って，もう一度大きな声で発表するように促す。
5. 全員が発表を終えたら，内容が一番おもしろかった生徒と発表が一番上手かった生徒の名前を投票用紙に書かせて提出させる。さらに自分の発表した文も清書用紙に書かせて提出させる。
6. 次の時間にそれぞれの部門で1位の生徒を発表する。

Example

①"I (don't) like 〜, because ...." の場合
　S1: I like English, because Steven is our teacher. He is kind and funny.
　S2: I don't like English, because Steven is our teacher. He gives us a lot of homework.

②"If I had a million dollars, ..." の場合
　S1: If I had a million dollars, I would travel all over the world with my friends.
　S2: If I had a million dollars, I would buy a pretty house and live with Bob, my dog.

ひとことコーナー

- 英文は他の生徒と少しでも違っていればよいことにすれば，英語が不得意な生徒でも積極的に参加できる。
- 生徒が清書した文を次回までにプリントして配布し，互いに読み合わせるとよい。

19. Speaking Competition

★　　　★　　　★

Students make one or two sentences using target grammar or key expressions, and then read them aloud to the class. A vote is taken to choose the speaker who made the best sentences, and the speaker who gave the best delivery.

Level: Beginner to Intermediate
Purpose: Speaking, Listening, Writing, Reading/Grammar, Key expressions
Materials: Voting paper and blank sheet for each student
Usage: Practice, Review
Time: *Preparation*—5 minutes　　*Activity*—20 to 30 minutes

● Description of Activity ●

1. Have students write down one or two sentences using target grammar or key expressions in their notebooks (see Example, p.76).

2. When the students finish writing their expressions, give a voting paper and a blank sheet (see p.78) to each one.

3. Demonstrate the activity.
   ①Students raise their hands and read out their sentences. A previous student's sentence must not be repeated.
   ②As there will be a vote for the speaker who made the most imaginative sentences (Today's Fun Speaker), and the one who gave the most impressive delivery (Today's Best Speaker), students should take notes in their notebooks.

4. Start the activity. Students raise their hands and read their sentences aloud in turn. Students will join in competitively, because the later they present their sentences, the greater the possibility that another student will have already used the same ones. If students speak too softly, have them repeat themselves in a loud voice by saying, "Please repeat that sentence."

5. Once the presentations have finished, have the students write the names of Today's Fun Speaker and Today's Best Speaker on the voting paper. Students write down their own sentences on the blank sheet and give this to the teacher.

6. In the next class announce the names of Today's Fun Speaker and Today's Best Speaker.

Additional Information

- A slight difference in sentence construction will be satisfactory. In this way, less able students will be more motivated to join in.
- By the next lesson, type up all the students' sentences and then give each of them a copy in class.

19. Speaking Competition

A. 投票用紙(Voting Paper)の記入例

> I think Today's Fun Speaker is
>   <u>Koyama Akira</u>.
> Today's Best Speaker is
>   <u>Suzuki Risa</u>.

B. 清書用紙(Blank Sheet)の記入例

> If I had a million dollars, I would go to Mars and live there with Brad Pitt.
> Class <u>2</u> Name <u>Mori Asako</u>

A. 投票用紙(Voting Paper)

> I think Today's Fun Speaker is
>   _____ .
>
> Today's Best Speaker is
>   _____ .

B. 清書用紙(Blank Sheet)

> _____
> _____
> _____
> _____
>
> Class _____ Name _____

MEMO

ACTIVITY 20 Find the Whole Story

教師が読む話を聞いた後でその内容を書いて再現し，どれだけ正確に聞き取れたかをグループ同士で競う活動。

Level: 初級～上級
Purpose: Listening, Writing
Materials: 読み物教材等から抜粋した英文，メモ用紙(生徒数分)，まとめ用の用紙(グループ数分)
Usage: 定期試験後の授業等での投げ込み教材として
Time: 準備—20分　　活動—15～20分

● Description of Activity ●

1. クラスを4～6人ずつのグループに分け，机を移動してグループごとにつけさせる。
2. 生徒全員にメモ用紙を配布する。また，各グループにまとめ用の用紙を1枚ずつ配布する。
3. 教師は教材を読み，生徒に聞かせる。生徒は聞きながらメモ用紙にできるだけたくさんの情報を書き留める。
4. 聞き終わったらグループごとに各メンバーの情報を寄せ集め，できるだけ話の全体像に近づけていく。
5. 各グループの代表が自分のグループがまとめた話を読み上げ，どのグループが一番よく聞き取れたかを教師が判定する。

▶NOTE　教師が生徒に教材を聞かせる回数は，生徒の理解の様子を見ながら判断する。

ひとことコーナー

・予習を前提としている授業では，聞き取り用の教材に教科書を使うのは避けたほうがよい。
・教材には，数字(日付など)や固有名詞(人名，地名など)が含まれているものがよい。グループごとのまとめの内容に差が出てきて活動が盛り上がる。生徒のレベルに合わせて，ALTに教材を書いてもらってもよい。

20. Find the Whole Story

★   ★   ★

After listening to a story, groups of students compete to recreate it in written form as precisely as possible.

Level: Beginner to Advanced
Purpose: Listening, Writing
Materials: Passage for reading, Paper for notetaking for each student, Paper for recreating the passage for each group
Usage: Deviation from the textbook after an exam or a series of lessons
Time: *Preparation*—20 minutes   *Activity*—15 to 20 minutes

● **Description of Activity** ●

1. Divide the class into groups of four to six students. Have each group move their desks and sit together.
2. Give each student a piece of paper for notetaking. Give each group an additional piece of paper for writing their group's story.
3. Read aloud some new material to the class. Each student writes down as much of the passage as possible while they are listening.
4. Group members pool their knowledge to recreate the passage on the additional sheet of paper as precisely as possible.
5. A representative from each group reads its version aloud to the class. Judge which group has written the most accurate reconstruction.

▶**NOTE** Read the passage aloud to the students more than once if necessary.

Additional Information

- It would be inappropriate to use the textbook as the source of the reading material where students are in the habit of preparing for lessons by reading ahead: alternative material should be used.
- If passages containing numbers (such as dates) and proper nouns (for example, names of people and cities) are used, then students will find the activity more challenging. Have the ALT prepare a passage appropriate to the students' level.

ACTIVITY 21

Some Tips for Reading Aloud

学年が進むにつれて生徒の音読の声は小さくなる。音読を成功に導くあの手この手を紹介する。

Level: 初級〜上級
Purpose: Reading, Listening, Speaking
Materials: 教科書，テープ，音読用プリント，評価表
Usage: 授業の中での活動(各授業時に毎回帯状に入れる)
Time: 準備—0〜5分　活動—5〜10分

● Description of Activity ●

1. **Pause Reading**
    センス・グループごとに区切りながら教科書の本文を音読する。生徒は各自の教科書にポーズ・マーク(／など)をつけながら，教師の後について音読していく。

2. **Read and Look Up**
    生徒に最初のセンス・グループを黙読する時間を与える。教師が "Look up." と言ったら，生徒は顔を上げて黙読した部分を言う。センス・グループごとにこの活動を続けていく。一通り文章全体の読みが終わったら，1文ごとに行ってもよい。

3. **Pair Reading**
    一斉読み，個別読みを行った後で，生徒をペアにしてお互いの音読を聞かせる。その時，より自然な聴きとりになるように，うなずいたり，"really", "erm", "uh-huh", "And then …?" などの相づちを打つ活動を行わせるとよい(『言語活動成功事例集』p.74, 23. Conversation Reading 参照)。

4. **Simultaneous Reading**
    教科書に準拠したテープと同時に音読する。LL教室で行うか，またはヘッドフォン・ステレオを用いることができれば，より効果的である。

5. **Simultaneous Reading with Blanked Texts**
    文章中のいくつかの語や句を空欄にしてあるプリントを用意し，生徒はそれを見て空欄を補いながら，テープと同時に音読する。

6. **Chain Reading or Relay Reading**
    決められた分量(1文，2文，1段落など)の文を，次々に指名された生徒が音読していく。指名するのは生徒でも教師でもよい。指名された生徒は，どこから読むかわからない場合は "Please read the last (two) sentence(s) again." などのように言って聞き返す。聞かれた生徒はもう一度最後の1，2文をクラス中に聞こえるように読む。

7. **音読カードの利用**
    音読カード(p.85参照)を作り，生徒に配っておく。音読するたびに，各自に音読の回数等を記録させる。教師は時々点検し，評価し，激励する。

8. **暗唱のすすめ**
    音読を何度もした後で，生徒は1人ずつ教師のところに行き，1段落だけでもよいから教科書なしで暗唱するようにする。教師は評価とコメントをそれぞれのカードに記録する。

21. Some Tips for Reading Aloud

ひとことコーナー

- 音読の大切さはわかっていても，高学年になるにつれて生徒は声を出さなくなる。その理由は，一つには言語材料が難しくなること，もう一つには人前で大きな声を出すことを恥ずかしがる精神的な年齢になることが挙げられよう。しかし，ここで紹介した方法なら，高学年でも音読に興味を持たせることができる。
- 暗唱の評価を平常点として加えることにすると，生徒は意欲的に取り組む。

★ ★ ★

Some techniques to overcome students' reluctance to read aloud in class as they grow older.

Level: Beginner to Advanced
Purpose: Reading, Listening, Speaking
Materials: Textbook, Tape, Reading Aloud Evaluation Card
Usage: Practice (A regular slot in each class)
Time: *Preparation*—0 to 5 minutes   *Activity*—5 to 10 minutes

● Description of Activity ●

1. **Pause Reading**
   Read aloud to the class, pausing after each "sense group." Students repeat aloud, and make a slash mark in their textbook after each such group.

2. **Read and Look Up**
   Give students time to read the first sense group silently. Say "Look up"; the students do so and say out loud what they have just read. Once the whole passage has been read in this way, repeat using complete sentences instead of sense groups.

3. **Pair Reading**
   Have students read the entire passage chorally and individually. Next, have students in pairs take turns in listening to each other read aloud. While one student reads, their partner should use nods of the head, and expressions such as "really", "erm", "uh-huh", "And then...?" and so on, at appropriate moments to make the act of listening more natural. (See Activity 23, Conversation Reading, p.74, in *Communication Activities Book 1*).

4. **Simultaneous Reading**
   Have the students read aloud simultaneously with the tape that accompanies the textbook. If this is done in a language laboratory or using a personal stereo, the activity will be more effective.

5. **Simultaneous Reading with Blanked Text**
   Before class, prepare a handout of the passage in which there are some blanks. Students read aloud with the tape, verbally filling in the blanks.

6. **Chain Reading or Relay Reading**
   Have a student read aloud the first segment (sentence or paragraph) of the text, while their classmates listen. The teacher or the student chooses the next speaker, who reads the following segment, and so on. If an appointed student does not know from where to

21. Some Tips for Reading Aloud

continue, they say to the previous student, "Please read the last (two) sentence(s) again." The previous student does so.

7. **Use of Evaluation Cards**

   Give each student a Reading Aloud Evaluation Card (see p.85). Have the students complete this each time they read aloud. Check and comment on these from time to time, to encourage the students.

8. **Learning by Heart**

   After the students have read aloud many times, they should, individually, read aloud to the teacher, without using their textbooks, even if it's just a paragraph. Grade and comment upon their performance on the card.

Additional Information

- Although the importance of reading aloud is well known, students become less willing to do it as they grow older for two reasons: the reading material becomes more difficult, and they become embarrassed to speak aloud in front of others. These activities will help overcome their reluctance.
- If evaluation of the Learning by Heart phase is included in the students' assessments, they will be motivated to do well.

Reading Aloud Evaluation Card

音読カード

Class _____   Name _____

月／日	ページ	音読回数	自己評価	教師の評価
5／10	p. 16	3回	B	Good!
5／13	p. 17	5回	A	Great!

※自己評価はA，B，C，D，Eの5段階

ACTIVITY 22 Let's Be a Cartoonist! ①

4コママンガのせりふを英語に訳す活動。

Level: 中級～上級
Purpose: Writing, Speaking
Materials: ワークシート
Usage: 定期試験後の授業等での投げ込み教材として
Time: 準備―5～20分　活動―15～30分

● Description of Activity ●

1. 生徒全員にワークシート (pp.87-89参照) を配る。
2. 各自に4コママンガの日本語のせりふをふさわしい英語に訳させ，吹き出しに書き込ませる。
3. 数人の生徒に発表させる。

ひとことコーナー
- 新聞の4コママンガを使うと教材はいくつでも作れる。
- この活動はグループで行ってもよい。

★　　　★　　　★

Students translate comic strips into English.

Level: Intermediate to Advanced
Purpose: Writing, Speaking
Materials: Worksheet
Usage: Deviation from the textbook after an exam or a series of lessons
Time: *Preparation*—5 to 20 minutes　*Activity*—15 to 30 minutes

● Description of Activity ●

1. Give a worksheet (see pp.87-89) to each student.
2. Have the students translate the dialogue into English and write it into the empty speech bubbles.
3. Have some of the students present their dialogues to their classmates.

Additional Information
- By keeping the comic strips printed in newspapers, it is possible to accumulate a lot of material quickly.
- This activity can be undertaken in a group.

Worksheet 1

Let's Be a Cartoonist！①

Class _____ Name _____

アサッテ君
東海林さだお
（9106）

Panel 1: 早く顔洗わないとまにあわないわよー

Panel 2: 顔洗うのめんどくさいなー

Panel 3: 洗わないでいい　無洗米

Panel 4: 洗わないでいい　無洗顔 ／ うるさいッ

毎日新聞（2001年3月6日付）

※このワークシートは拡大して使ってください。／Please enlarge this worksheet.

Worksheet 2

Let's Be a Cartoonist! ①

Class _____   Name _____

Worksheet 3

Let's Be a Cartoonist! ①

Class _____   Name _____

アサッテ君
東海林さだお
（9183）

Panel 1: 朝のこない夜はない

Panel 2: 出口のないトンネルはない

Panel 3: すこし元気が出てきたよ / うん

Panel 4: カロリーのない食べ物はない

毎日新聞（2001年5月25日付）

※このワークシートは拡大して使ってください。／Please enlarge this worksheet.

ACTIVITY 23 Let's Be a Cartoonist! ②

2コマ程度のマンガを見て,場面や状況に合うせりふを考える活動。

Level: 中級~上級
Purpose: Writing, Speaking
Materials: ワークシート
Usage: 定期試験後の授業等での投げ込み教材として
Time: 準備—5~20分 活動—15~30分

● **Description of Activity** ●

1. 生徒全員にワークシート(p.91参照)を配る。
2. 各自にマンガの場面や状況にふさわしい英語のせりふを考えさせ,吹き出しに書き込ませる。
3. 数人の生徒に発表させる。

ひとことコーナー

- この種のマンガ教材は生徒に描いてもらうとよい。「このクラスでマンガの上手い人は誰?」と尋ねると,すぐに2,3人の名前があがるはずである。そういう生徒に頼むと簡単にしかも立派な教材ができあがる。
- この活動はグループで行ってもよい。

★   ★   ★

Students create their own dialogues for simple comic strips.

Level: Intermediate to Advanced
Purpose: Writing, Speaking
Materials: Worksheet
Usage: Deviation from the textbook after an exam or a series of lessons
Time: *Preparation*—5 to 20 minutes *Activity*—15 to 30 minutes

● **Description of Activity** ●

1. Give a worksheet (see p.91) to each student.
2. Each student thinks of suitable English dialogue for the comic strips and writes it in the speech bubbles.
3. Have some of the students present their dialogues to their classmates.

23. Let's Be a Cartoonist! ②

Additional Information

- Have some of the students draw the comic strips. If the class is asked who its best comic strip artists are, two or three names will be suggested. Such students can provide the teacher with good material.
- This activity can also be done in a group.

Worksheet

Let's Be a Cartoonist! ②

Class _____ Name _____

1

2

※このワークシートは拡大して使ってください。／Please enlarge this worksheet.

ACTIVITY 24

What's Happened?

ある場面の前後を描いた2コマの絵を見て，その間に何が起こったか想像し，英語で発表する活動。

Level: 中級〜上級
Purpose: Writing, Speaking
Materials: ワークシート
Usage: 定期試験後の授業等での投げ込み教材として
Time: 準備—20分　　活動—15〜30分

● Description of Activity ●

1. 生徒全員に，2コマの絵を描いたワークシート(p.93参照)を配る。2コマの絵は，それぞれある場面の「前」と「後」を表している。
2. 2コマの絵を見て，その間に何が起こったかを考えさせ，ワークシートに書かせる。
3. 数人の生徒に発表させる。

ひとことコーナー

・この種の教材は生徒に描いてもらうと活動に活気が出てよい。
・レベルを上げるには，2でワークシートに書かせずに，口頭発表させるとよい。
・この活動を発展させたものとして，最初の1枚の絵だけを見せて，「この後に起こることを考えなさい」という活動も考えられる。
・この活動はグループで行ってもよい。

★　　　★　　　★

Students look at a "before" and "after" picture and imagine what has taken place.

Level: Intermediate to Advanced
Purpose: Writing, Speaking
Materials: Worksheet
Usage: Deviation from the textbook after an exam or a series of lessons
Time: *Preparation*—20 minutes　　*Activity*—15 to 30 minutes

● Description of Activity ●

1. Give a worksheet (see p.93) to each student. The pictures on it comprise a "before" and "after" sequence.
2. Have the students look at the pictures and think about what has happened between them.
3. Have some of the students present their thoughts to the class.

24. What's Happened?

Additional Information

- Using pictures drawn by some of the students will motivate the class.
- It will be easier for students to make their presentations from notes they have made. However, if students must present without notes, the activity will be more challenging.
- As a variation on this activity, let students see the first picture only. They must then imagine what happens next.
- This activity can be done in a group.

Worksheet

What's Happened?

Class _____ Name_____

A (Before)   ▶   B (After)

What's happened between A and B?

93

ACTIVITY 25

Who's Who?

> 与えられた絵のなかの7人の人物がそれぞれ誰であるか，教室の壁に貼られた手がかり (clue cards) から情報を集め，グループで人物を特定していく活動。

Level: 中級～上級
Purpose: Speaking, Reading, Listening, Writing
Materials: 9枚のclue cards，ワークシート，メモ用紙(それぞれグループ数分)
Usage: 定期試験後の授業等での投げ込み教材として
Time: 準備―10分　活動―30～40分

● Description of Activity ●

1. あらかじめ9枚のclue cards (p.97参照) をB5判程度の大きさの紙に拡大しておき，授業前に教室の壁にバラバラに貼りつけておく。
2. 生徒を5，6人ずつのグループに分け，机を移動してグループごとにつけさせる。
3. 各グループにChief Detectiveとなるリーダーを1人決めさせ，その生徒にワークシート(p.96参照)とメモ用紙を1枚ずつ配布する。
4. 活動について説明する。
   ①Chief Detective以外のメンバーはDetectivesとなって教室内を走り回り，壁に貼られている9枚のclue cardsを読んで記憶し(メモをとってはいけない)，それをグループに戻ってChief Detectiveに伝える。
   ②Chief Detectiveは自分の席を離れずにDetectivesが取ってきたすべての情報をメモ用紙に記録する。
   ③Chief Detectiveは記録した情報をもとに，Detectivesと相談しながらワークシートを完成させていく。
5. 活動開始。わからなくなったら，Detectivesはいつでもclue cardsの内容を確認しに行ってよい。
6. ワークシートを完成させたら，Chief Detectiveは教師のところに持っていく。最初に正解したグループが勝ちとなる。

ひとことコーナー

- 活動に入る前に，職業名などの未習の語について説明しておくとよい。
- 各グループに辞書を用意しておき，わからない語・語句があれば調べさせる方法もある。
- 教師は，cluesを見に走り回る生徒がいつも限られてしまわないように注意する。

25. Who's Who?

★   ★   ★

> By getting information from clue cards fixed to the walls of the classroom, students identify the seven people in a picture.

Level: Intermediate to Advanced
Purpose: Speaking, Reading, Listening, Writing
Materials: Nine clue cards, Worksheet and blank B5 sheet for each group
Usage: Deviation from the textbook after an exam or a series of lessons
Time: *Preparation*—10 minutes   *Activity*—30 to 40 minutes

● **Description of Activity** ●

1. Before class, enlarge each of the nine clue cards (see p.97) to about B5 size and fix them to the classroom walls.
2. Divide the students into groups of five or six. Have each group move their desks and sit together.
3. Have each group select a leader, the Chief Detective. Give a worksheet (see p.96) and a blank B5 sheet to the Chief Detective of each group.
4. Demonstrate the activity to the students.
   ①Apart from the Chief Detective, all group members are Detectives. The Detectives go around the room to read and memorize the clues. The Detectives, who are not allowed to write anything down, tell the clues to the Chief Detective.
   ②The Chief Detectives must remain seated at their desks, and write down the clues that the Detectives tell them on their blank sheets.
   ③The Chief Detectives complete the worksheets, working together with the Detectives.
5. Start the activity. If necessary, the Detectives can go back to check the clues.
6. The students take their completed worksheets to the teacher. The first group to arrive at the correct solution is the winner.

Additional Information
- Be sure to teach any new vocabulary—such as the job titles—before starting the activity.
- You can also give a dictionary to each group and encourage students to use them.
- Ensure that all the students are engaged in the activity.

Worksheet

Who's Who?

Group No. _____

Here's a picture of the Ashton family: Ada, Alice, Bill, George, Karen, Mabel and Steven—but who's who? How old are they? What are their jobs?

Name (名前), Age (年齢) について書き入れなさい。

Name	Age	Job
		Artist
		Journalist
		Scientist
		Taxi Driver
		Teacher
		Nurse
		Tour Guide

Clue Cards

George is twice as old as Ada.	Bill is half as old as Mabel, who can't drive.
Ada, who is two years older than Bill, takes people sightseeing.	Karen paints.
Karen is five years younger than Steven.	Alice, who writes for a newspaper, is six years older than Karen.
Ada is four years older than Alice.	The oldest person works in a laboratory.
Steven, who works in a school, is 25.	**Solution** Karen — 20 — Artist Alice — 26 — Journalist George — 60 — Scientist Bill — 28 — Taxi Driver Steven — 25 — Teacher Mabel — 56 — Nurse Ada — 30 — Tour Guide

ACTIVITY 26

Look! I'm on TV!

グループで身の回りにある物のテレビ・コマーシャルを作り，発表する活動。

Level: 中級～上級
Purpose: Speaking, Listening, Writing
Materials: 身の回りのさまざまな物
Usage: 定期試験後等の投げ込み教材として
Time: 準備―5～10分　　活動―50分

● Description of Activity ●

1. クラスを4，5人ずつのグループに分け，机を移動してグループごとにつけさせる。
2. 身の回りのさまざまな物(例えば，携帯電話，目覚まし時計，靴，ユニークな洋服，椅子，など)を教室の前の方に並べ，これから各グループで1つの物を選び，それについてのテレビ・コマーシャルを作ってクラス全員の前で発表すると伝える。
3. グループの代表にコマーシャルをする物を選ばせる。各グループはそれぞれ異なる物を選ばなければならない。
4. 生徒にルールを説明する。
   ①コマーシャルの長さは約1分間。
   ②グループの全員が話さなくていけない。
5. コマーシャルを作る時間として約25分間与える。
6. 各グループに順番にコマーシャルを発表させる。
7. 最後にどのグループが一番上手だったかを，クラス全員の挙手で決める。

▶NOTE　この活動に入る前に教師がコマーシャルのモデルを示すこと。できるだけおもしろいコマーシャルがよい(p.100, Example Commercial for Teachers' Demonstration 参照)。
　　　　生徒は自分たちのコマーシャル作りに熱中するため，他のグループの発表を聞かないことがある。聞かせるためには，机を元に戻し，全員に前を向かせる。

ひとことコーナー
・授業のはじめに2グループずつ発表させ，ウォームアップとすることも可能である。この場合は最も上手なグループを選ぶことはできない。

26. Look! I'm on TV!

★   ★   ★

Students in groups act out their own TV commercials for everyday objects.

Level: Intermediate to Advanced
Purpose: Speaking, Listening, Writing
Materials: Various objects
Usage: Deviation from the textbook after an exam or a series of lessons
Time: *Preparation*—5 to 10 minutes   *Activity*—50 minutes

● Description of Activity ●

1. Have the students make groups of four or five. Have each group move their desks and sit together.
2. Have a number of objects on display at the front of the class, such as a mobile phone, an alarm clock, a pair of shoes, an unusual item of clothing, a chair, and so on. Tell the class that each group is going to make its own television commercial for one of the objects and then act it out in front of the class.
3. Have a representative from each group claim their object. Each group must choose something different.
4. Explain the rules.
   ①Each commercial must last for about a minute.
   ②Every member of the group must speak during the commercial.
5. Allow the class about 25 minutes for preparation.
6. Have the groups take turns in presenting their commercials to the class.
7. Students vote for the best commercial on a show of hands, but may not choose their own.

▶**NOTE**   If you can demonstrate your own example commercial to the students at the beginning of the lesson, particularly in a team-taught class, this will act as a great motivator— the funnier the better! See Example Commercial for Teachers' Demonstration (p.100).
   When students are performing, ensure that the other groups are watching and not continuing with their own preparations.

Additional Information
· As an alternative to step 6, rather than having students perform in the same lesson in which they carry out preparation, have two groups present their commercials as the warm-up in the next few lessons and ignore step 7.

26. Look! I'm on TV!

Example Commercial for Teachers' Demonstration

The ALT is holding an old, shabby supermarket carrier bag.

ALT: Look at this! It's my *Superbag*!
JTE: Great colors!
ALT: It's very strong!
JTE: It's so cool!
ALT: I can carry my school books!
JTE: You can carry your lunch!
ALT: I can carry a lot of things!
JTE: How much is it?
ALT: It's not 100,000 yen. It's not 10,000 yen. It's not 1,000 yen. It's ... 100 yen!
JTE: Wow! Only 100 yen!
ALT and JTE*: Great colors! Very strong! Looks so cool! Wow! Wow! Buy one now!

* *To be said rythmically at a fast tempo*

MEMO

ACTIVITY 27 Repairing Broken Sentences

カードに書かれたキーワードを用いて相手に質問し，答えた相手にさらに質問をして対話を続けていく活動。

Level: 中級〜上級
Purpose: Speaking, Listening
Materials: キーワードが書いてあるカード
Usage: ウォームアップ，授業中での活動，復習
Time: 準備―10分　活動―15〜20分

● Description of Activity ●

1. あらかじめ，キーワードの書いてあるカード(p.103, Example Broken Sentence Cards 参照)を作り，各ペアに1組ずつ分用意する。カードはすぐに使えるよう，1枚ずつバラバラに切り離しておく。
2. 生徒にペアを組ませ，机をつけさせる。一方をA，他方をBとする。
3. 各ペアにカードを1組ずつ配り，机の上に裏返しに重ねて置かせる。
4. Aは一番上のカードをめくり，カードに書かれたキーワードを用いてBに質問する。例えば，go / London が出たとすると，Bに対する質問は "Do you want to go to London?" あるいは "Have you ever been to London?" などが考えられる。動詞の時制や名詞の単数・複数などは適当に変えてよいことにする。さらに形容詞や副詞なども自由に挿入して構わない。
5. BはAの質問に答える。AはBの答えに基づいてさらに質問をし，Bはそれに答える(Example Conversation 参照)。
6. 役割を交替し，次のカードで活動を続けていく。

Example Conversation

    A: Have you ever been to London?
    B: No, but I'm going there this summer.
    A: Great! Alone?
    B: Ah! That's a secret!

ひとことコーナー

- 「質問はすべて過去形でする」とか「必ず副詞を含んだ質問にする」などのように，さまざまな条件を与えることで，特定の表現を練習させたり活動のレベルを上げたりすることができる。

27. Repairing Broken Sentences

★ ★ ★

> Each student asks their partner a question that they have made up using two or more keywords. Their partner answers, and a follow-up question is asked.
>
> **Level:** Intermediate to Advanced
> **Purpose:** Speaking, Listening
> **Materials:** Set of Broken Sentence Cards for each student
> **Usage:** Warm-up, Practice, Review
> **Time:** *Preparation*—10 minutes   *Activity*—15 to 20 minutes

● Description of Activity ●

1. Before class, prepare a set of Broken Sentence Cards for each pair of students (see the examples below). Cut out each card.
2. In class, have the students make pairs and move their desks together: one student is A, and the other is B.
3. Give each pair a set of cards. They should be placed in a pile face down on the desk.
4. A turns over the top card and asks B a question made up from the keywords on it. For example, the "go / London" card might generate "Do you want to go to London?" or "Have you ever been to London?" Students are free to change the tense of verbs on the cards, use singular or plural forms, and insert adjectives and adverbs.
5. B answers. A asks a follow-up question based on B's answer. B replies. See Example Conversation (p. 102).
6. A and B change roles and the activity continues with the next card.

Additional Information
- The teacher can impose restrictions to practice particular language or to make the activity more challenging: for example, all questions must be in the past tense, or all questions must include an adverb.

Example Broken Sentence Cards

go / London	weather / tomorrow
what / hobbies	how many / brothers / sisters
where / go / holiday	job / like / do

ACTIVITY 28

Who's My Special Friend?

各自に配られたワークシートに書かれている情報をもとに，他の生徒に質問しながらそのワークシートに記入した人(Special Friend)を探す活動。

Level: 初級〜中級
Purpose: Speaking, Listening, Writing
Materials: ワークシート
Usage: 授業中での活動(特にクラス開きの時)
Time: 準備—10分　活動—30〜50分

● Description of Activity ●

1. 生徒全員にワークシート(p.106参照)を配り，各自のワークシートの質問に自分なりの答えを書かせる。他の生徒に見られないようにさせ，名前も書かないように指示する。
2. 全員のワークシートを集めてよく切り，あらためて1枚ずつ生徒に配る。自分の書いたワークシートが配られた場合は教師に戻させ，他の生徒のものと交換する。
3. 活動開始。生徒は自分のSpecial Friend(手に持っているワークシートを書いた人)を探していく。このため，まず立ってペアになり，互いに質問し合う。そして，ワークシートの情報を基に相手が自分のSpecial Friendであるかどうか判断する。質問はどのような順番でも構わない。また，ワークシートのすべての質問をする必要はない。相手が自分のSpecial Friendでないとわかり，相手の質問に答え終わったら，別の生徒を見つけて質問をする。
4. Special Friendを見つけた生徒は自分の席に座るが，そのSpecial Friend自身は自分のSpecial Friendを見つけるまで活動を続ける。探しているSpecial Friendがすでに座っている場合もあるので注意させる。
5. 全員がSpecial Friendを見つけた時点で活動を終了する。自分のSpecial Friendについて，ワークシートの情報を使いながら発表させる(Example Introduction参照)。

Example Introduction

　　I'll introduce Yukari. She lives in Tsukuba. She has one sister. She's called Eri. Yukari is in the tennis club. She says her favorite subject is English, but I don't believe her! She likes *Titanic* because it's exciting, romantic and sad! She loves English food! She sends e-mail to someone in London called Alice. Yukari wants to go to England to meet her. Thank you.

▶**NOTE** 生徒には，ワークシートに書かれている質問の表現を，自分なりに変えてみるように勧める。例えば，"Which town or city are you from?" の質問に "Tokyo." と書かれたシートを持っていたら，"Do you come from Tokyo?" のように表現を変えさせる。

🎵ひとことコーナー
・あらかじめワークシートに番号をふり，生徒にその番号をおぼえておかせると混乱が起こらない。
・ALTとのTTの場合や大人数クラスでは，クラスを2つに分けて活動させるとよい。
・大人数のクラスでは発表に時間がかかるので，生徒にはSpecial Friendの名前の他に1つだけ面白い情報を選ばせて発表させるとよい。例えば，"This is Yukari. She wants to go to England to meet her e-mail friend, Alice."

28. Who's My Special Friend?

★   ★   ★

Students anonymously complete worksheets with personal information. These are randomly redistributed, and students have to find their Special Friends by asking questions.

Level: Beginner to Intermediate
Purpose: Speaking, Listening, Writing
Materials: Worksheet
Usage: Practice (Introduction activity for new students)
Time: *Preparation*—10 minutes   *Activity*—30 to 50 minutes

● Description of Activity ●

1. Give a worksheet (see p.106) to each student. Have them complete them. They should not let other students know what they are writing. They should not write their names on the sheets.

2. Collect the worksheets. Shuffle them thoroughly, and then give one back to each student. If a student receives their own worksheet back, exchange it for another one. Students should not be aware whose worksheet they have.

3. Start the activity. Each student has to find their Special Friend — this is the student who completed the worksheet they are holding. To do this, they start by standing and pairing off. They take turns to ask each other questions, and by using the information on the worksheets, they decide whether or not their partners are their Special Friends. Questions can be asked in any order. Students don't have to ask every question on the worksheet. As soon as a student realizes that their partner is not their Special Friend, and provided they have answered their partner's questions, they find another classmate to question.

4. Students sit down when they have identified their Special Friends, while their Special Friends remain standing and must continue to look for *their* Special Friends. *Students should remember that their Special Friends may be sitting down.*

5. When all the students have found their Special Friends, have them introduce them to the class, using the information on the worksheets. See the Example Introduction (p.104).

▶ **NOTE** Encourage students to make their own questions. For example, if the answer to the worksheet question, "Which town or city are you from?" is "Tokyo," a student can ask "Do you come from Tokyo?"

Additional Information

- Before class, number each worksheet. Have students remember the number of the worksheet they completed, in order to reduce possible confusion.
- In team-taught classes or in large classes, divide the students into groups of no more than 20 members, or else the activity will take too long to complete.
- In large classes, in step 5 have students choose just one interesting piece of information about their Special Friends: for example, "This is Yukari. She wants to go to England to meet her e-mail friend, Alice."

Worksheet

No. _____

- Which town or city are you from?
- Which club do you belong to?
- What country would you like to visit and why?
- How many brothers and sisters do you have?
- What subject do you like best?
- What are the names of your brothers and sisters?
- What movie do you like best?
- What Western food do you like best?

MEMO

ACTIVITY 29　What Do You Think?

トピックカードに書かれた質問や文を話のきっかけにして，小グループで自由に会話や討論をする活動。

Level: 　　中級〜上級
Purpose: 　Speaking, Listening
Materials: トピックカード
Usage: 　　授業中での活動
Time: 　　準備—10分　　活動—30分

● **Description of Activity** ●

1. クラスを3，4人ずつのグループに分け，机を移動してグループごとにつけさせる。
2. 各グループにあらかじめバラバラに切っておいたトピックカード (pp.110-111参照) を1組ずつ与え，裏返しに重ねて机の上に置かせる。
3. グループの1人が一番上のカードをめくる。書かれている質問をきっかけとして，グループの誰かが最初に自分の意見を言う。それに対して，他のメンバーは自分の賛成意見や反対意見を自由に述べ，ディスカッションへと発展させる (Example of the Start of a Discussion 参照)。
4. 最初のトピックについてのディスカッションが終了したとグループで判断したら，次のカードへと移っていく。

Example of the Start of a Discussion
　Topic: You have won a million yen! What will you do?
　　A: I'll buy a house.
　　B: You need more than a million yen to buy a house!
　　A: I'll buy a doll's house!
　　B: Huh! I'm going to have a vacation with my friends.
　　C: Where will you go?
　　B: Errrm ... Britain.
　　C: Why?
　　B: I want to meet Queen Elizabeth.
　　A: She won't want to meet you!

▶**NOTE**　1つのトピックに対する時間の制限はない。どのグループも自分たちのグループにあったやり方で進めればよい。
　　会話やディスカッションがトピックからはずれても一向に構わない。それらを続けられることがこの活動の目的である。

ひとことコーナー
- 生徒は自分の本当の気持ちや意見を述べる必要はない。おもしろいアイディアやとんちんかんな意見もおおいに歓迎される。
- 1人の生徒が会話を独占せず，生徒全員が活発に参加できるように教師は配慮する。

29. What Do You Think?

★ ★ ★

Students in small groups have free conversation or discussion prompted by questions or statements given to them on Topic Cards.

Level: Intermediate to Advanced
Purpose: Speaking, Listening
Materials: Set of topic cards for each group
Usage: Practice
Time: *Preparation*—10 minutes   *Activity*—30 minutes

● Description of Activity ●

1. Divide the class into groups of three or four students. Have each group move their desks and sit together.
2. Each group is given a set of topic cards (see pp. 110-111) which should have been cut out before class. These are placed in a pile, face down, on a desk.
3. The topic card on the top of the pile is turned over. The question on it is used as a starting point for a discussion. One student expresses their opinion. Group members agree or disagree, stating and explaining their views. See Example of the Start of a Discussion (p. 108).
4. When the group decides that its discussion has ended, the next card is turned over and the procedure is repeated, starting with a different student.

▶ **NOTE**   There is no limit on the time that should be spent on each topic. Therefore, different groups will work their way through a different number of cards.
   It is perfectly acceptable if the conversations deviate from the topic: the purpose of this activity is to encourage conversation and discussion.

Additional Information

- Students do not have to express their real opinions. They are free to invent any point of view they wish.
- The teacher should ensure that all students actively participate. No student should be allowed to monopolize the discussion.

29. What Do You Think?

Topic Cards

What's your favorite TV program / movie / book and why?	What do you want to be in the future?
What's your favorite subject at school and why?	What do you think about the school uniform?

29. What Do You Think?

You have won a million yen! What will you do?	You have won a date with a famous person. Who will you choose and why?
Where do you want to go on vacation and why?	Who is your favorite singer and why?

ACTIVITY 30

Balloon Game

気球に異常が起こり，乗っている人のうち誰か1人が飛び降りて気球を軽くしないと，墜落して全員死ぬ危険がある。さて，誰が飛び降りるべきか。説得力がものを言うサバイバル・ゲーム。

Level: 中級〜上級
Purpose: Speaking, Listening, Writing
Materials: 名札用の厚めの用紙，理由を書くためのメモ用紙(それぞれ生徒数分)
Usage: 授業の中での活動
Time: 準備—10分　　活動—40〜50分

● Description of Activity ●

1. クラスを5，6人ずつのグループに分け，机を移動してグループごとにつけさせる。
2. 生徒全員に，現在生きていて，有名で，かつ尊敬されている人物を1人心に思い浮かべさせる。
3. その人物の名札を作り，他の生徒からよく見えるように机の上に立てさせる。
4. 生徒に次のような状況を伝える。
   「あなたは名札に書かれている有名人です。今，あなたたちは気球に乗っていますが，どうしても気球を軽くしないと墜落して全員が死亡する運命にあります。そのため，誰か1人気球から飛び降りてもらわなくてはなりません。誰が飛び降りるのか決めてください。」
5. 生徒は，自分が飛び降りるべきでない理由を2，3分で考え，メモ用紙に書く。
6. 生徒はそれぞれ自分の主張を，順次グループの仲間に発表していく。この主張は1人1分間で行う。他の生徒はメモを取る。グループ全員が終わったら，今度は互いの反論を1，2分間行う。その後に，誰が気球から飛び降りるべきかをグループで話し合って決める。
7. 各グループの代表は，飛び降りるべき人物とその理由をクラスに発表する。

30. Balloon Game

★   ★   ★

> The students are in a falling hot-air balloon. One of them must jump from it to save the other passengers. Students exercise their powers of persuasion and practice some debating skills in this survival activity.
>
> **Level:**   Intermediate to Advanced
> **Purpose:**   Speaking, Listening, Writing
> **Materials:** Blank name card and sheet of paper for each student
> **Usage:**   Practice
> **Time:**   *Preparation*—10 minutes   *Activity*—40 to 50 minutes

● Description of Activity ●

1. Divide the class into groups of five or six students. Have each group move their desks and sit together.
2. Each student must think of someone famous, alive today, who is respected.
3. Each student writes the name they have chosen on their name card and places it in front of them, so it can be seen by the other students.
4. Describe the following situation to the students.
   "Each of you is the famous person named on your card. You are in a balloon with the other members of your group. The balloon is falling. If it isn't made lighter, it will crash and everyone will die. So one person from your group must jump from the balloon. The group has to decide who this should be."
5. Students are given a few minutes to think of a reason why their character should not jump, and write it down.
6. The members of each group present their arguments to their fellow members. Each student has one minute to present their case: all the other students in the guoup take notes. Once everyone has done this, group members are given a few minutes to cross-examine each other. Then they discuss who should jump.
7. A representative from each group announces to the class who was chosen in their group and why.

ACTIVITY 31

Simple Pair Debate

本格的なディベートに入る前の基礎となる活動。ある事物についてペアで好き・嫌いの理由を述べ合う。

Level: 中級〜上級
Purpose: Speaking, Listening
Materials: なし
Usage: 授業の中での活動
Time: 準備―なし　活動―20〜30分

● Description of Activity ●

1. 生徒にペアを組ませ，片方をA，もう一方をBとする。
2. Aの生徒たちはトピック(事物)を好む立場になり，Bの生徒たちは嫌う立場になると伝える。
3. トピックを1つ与える(Example Topics 参照)。
4. 1分間の時間を与え，生徒にそれぞれの立場で好き・嫌いの理由をできるだけ多く考えさせる。理由は適当にこじつけたものでも構わない。
5. AはBに向かって，ある物が好きな理由を "I like 〜 because …." のように述べる。
6. 次にBがAに向かって，同じ物が嫌いな理由を "I don't like 〜 because …." のように述べる。BはAの意見と関係のないことを述べて構わない。
7. 教師がストップと言うまで，各ペアは約1分間交互に意見を言い合う。
8. 新しいトピックを次々に与え，4〜7の活動を繰り返させる。

Example Topics

- Summer
- *Natto*
- School
- *Snow*
- *Karaoke*
- Studying English
- Oranges
- Mobile phones
- Living with my family
- *Name of a popular singer/actor/character/television show/movie/book/etc.*

Example Debate

Topic: Summer

A: I like summer because I can eat ice cream.
B: I don't like summer because we get lots of homework.
A: I like summer because we don't go to school for six weeks.
B: I don't like summer because the sun is bad for the skin.
A: I like summer because I can swim in the sea.
B: I don't like summer because there are cockroaches.
A: I like summer because the days are longer.
B: I don't like summer because I get tired easily.
A: I like summer because I always go on holiday with my family.
B: I don't like summer because I sweat a lot!

31. Simple Pair Debate

ひとことコーナー

- この活動はディベートで必要とされる理由づけの練習である。『言語活動成功事例集』の 32. Ping Pong Debate, 33. Two-minute Role-play, 34. Six-minute Debate, 35. Table Debate より先に行うことが望ましい。
- 好き・嫌いの理由を考える1分の間に理由をメモするよう指示しておくとよい。

★　　★　　★

As an introduction to debate, students in pairs give reasons for liking or disliking certain topics.

Level: Intermediate to Advanced
Purpose: Speaking, Listening
Materials: None
Usage: Practice
Time: *Preparation*—None   *Activity*—20 to 30 minutes

● Description of Activity ●

1. Have the students make pairs: one student is A, the other is B.
2. Tell the A's they will like the topic you are about to introduce, while the B's will not.
3. Introduce the topic (see Example Topics, p.114).
4. Give the students a minute to think of reasons to support their opinions: these do not have to be orthodox.
5. A states their opinion and reason to B in the form, "I like ~ because …."
6. B replies in the form, "I don't like ~ because …." What B says does not have to be related to A's argument. See the Example Debate (p.114).
7. The students continue exchanging arguments alternately for one minute.
8. Introduce a new topic, have the students change roles, and repeat steps 4 to 7.

Additional Information

- This activity gives students practice in developing their reasoning skills, which are, of course, used in debate. It is especially suited for use before the following activities that were described in *Communication Activities Book 1*, "32, Ping Pong Debate," "33, Two-minute Role-play," "34, Six-minute Debate" and "35, Table Debate."
- If students are free to make notes when thinking of reasons to back up their arguments, extend the time allowed for step 4.

ACTIVITY 32

Brainstorm

本格的なディベートに入る前の予備的な活動。ある命題について賛成・反対の理由を，ペアでできるだけ多く考え出す。

Level:	上級
Purpose:	Speaking, Listening
Materials:	メモ用紙
Usage:	授業の中での活動
Time:	準備―5分　　活動―50分

● Description of Activity ●

1. クラスを4人ずつのグループに分け，さらに各グループを2人ずつのペア(AとB，CとD)に分ける。2つのペアの間を少し開け，机を移動して付けさせる。
2. 生徒にメモ用紙を配る。黒板に命題を書く(p.118, Example Propositions 参照)。
3. 各ペアに5分間時間を与え，命題に賛成の理由をできるだけ多く考えさせる。生徒は one-word summary (p.118, Example One-Word Summaries 参照)の形でメモしなければならない。
4. 次にAとC，BとDがペアになり，3で得た one-word summary を使いながら互いに説明し合う。生徒は新しい理由を聞いたら，同様に one-word summary の形でメモに書き加える。このようにして，5分間で互いに理由を共有する。
5. グループの4人が机をつけ，全員が同じ理由を one-word summary の形で整理していることを確認する。
6. 教師は各グループに次々と理由を尋ね，発表させる。前に言われてしまった理由は繰り返せない。すべての理由が発表されたところで終了する。
7. 今度は命題に反対する立場で3～6の活動を繰り返す。

STEP 1～3

A	B
C	D

STEP 4

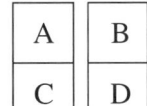

A	B
C	D

STEP 5, 6

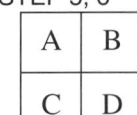

A	B
C	D

ひとことコーナー

・この活動はディベートで必要とされる理由づけをできるだけたくさん得るための方法である。また，one-word summary を見ながら相手に説明することにより，コミュニケーション活動へと導いている。
・この活動は，『言語活動成功事例集』32. Ping Pong Debate の後に行うことが望ましい。

32. Brainstorm

★   ★   ★

An introduction to one of the fundamental principles of debate. Students in pairs brainstorm to make as many arguments for and against a proposition as they can.

Level: Advanced
Purpose: Speaking, Listening
Materials: Paper for notetaking for each student
Usage: Practice
Time: *Preparation*—5 minutes   *Activity*—50 minutes

● **Description of Activity** ●

1. Have the students make groups of four, comprising Students A, B, C and D. A and B make a pair, as do C and D. Have each pair move their desks and sit together, but separately from the other pair.
2. Give each student a piece of paper for notetaking. Write the proposition on the board. (See Example Propositions, p.118.)
3. Give the students, working in their pairs, five minutes in which to think of as many separate arguments as possible in favor of the proposition. Each student must make their own (identical) list of their pair's arguments, writing down only *one word* for each argument. (See Example One-Word Summaries, p.118.)
4. Have the students change partners within their groups: so A pairs off with C, and B with D. Using their one-word summaries to help them, students take turns explaining their points to their new partners. Students add to their lists—again in one-word form—any new arguments that they hear. Allow five minutes for this.
5. All four group members sit together and make sure that each of them has all of their group's arguments listed in one-word summary form.
6. Ask the groups in turn to tell the class one of their arguments. Groups should not repeat arguments which have already been stated. Continue until all the separate arguments have been heard.
7. Repeat the procedure in steps 3 to 6 with groups making arguments against the proposition.

Additional Information

- This activity gives students practice in the essential debating skill of thinking of arguments to back up opinions. Having students explain themselves from one-word summaries leads to more natural and spontaneous communication than reading out written sentences (which would also have taken much longer to write).
- This activity would be a good one to use before "32, Ping Pong Debate" in *Communication Activities Book 1*.

32. Brainstorm

Example Propositions

- Dogs are better than cats.
- Radio is better than television.
- Futons are better than beds.
- Fast food and instant food are bad.
- It is better to be a man than a woman.
- Disposable wooden chopsticks should be banned.
- Students should be able to choose their teachers.
- High school students shouldn't have to wear school uniforms.
- English should be taught to Japanese people from kindergarten.
- Husbands and wives should be able to keep different surnames.
- The mobile phone is a bad invention.

Example One-Word Summaries

Proposition: Dogs are better than cats

Argument in favor	One-word summary
"Dogs are more friendly/loyal than cats…."	Friendly
"People get good exercise walking their dogs…."	Healthy
"Dogs can help blind people…."	Blind
"Dogs can help the police…."	Police

And so on.

MEMO

参 考 文 献

K. Johnson ／ K. Morrow 編著，小笠原八重訳 『コミュニカティブ・アプローチと英語教育』　桐原書店 (1984)

薬袋洋子　『英語教師の四十八手〈第7巻〉リーディングの指導』　研究社出版 (1994)

おわりに

　『言語活動成功事例集』を発刊したのが平成10年の初夏のことでした。その年の4月，私は埼玉県立南教育センター(現総合教育センター)から県立大宮光陵高等学校の教頭として転任しました。この学校は全国でも珍しく，音楽科・美術科・書道科という芸術科を普通科に併設する学校でした。覚悟はしていたものの，一日ほぼ12時間，学校運営の仕事に走り回る日々が始まりました。光陵高校での3年間，学校で英語に触れたことは全くありませんでした。本書は，そんな生活の中で週末を使ってコツコツと整理・執筆を進め，仕上げたものです。今，こうして発刊の運びとなり，過ぎ去った3年間の日々を感慨深く想い返しているところです。

　この4月(平成13年)，私は埼玉県立所沢養護学校の校長になりました。この学校は小・中・高の知的障害をもつ児童・生徒の教育にあたる学校で，武蔵野の林の中にひっそりと立つ学校です。今まで，学校では高校生としか会わなかった私ですが，現在，小学生から高校生まで毎日おつきあいしております。なんとも不思議な日々です。

　高校の英語教師として出発し，教育センターの外国語担当の指導主事，大宮光陵高等学校の教頭，そして，所沢養護学校の校長。本人の予測を超える自分の人生の展開に驚いております。反面，楽しんでもおります。今，私は，少しずつ，障害児教育にのめり込み始めました。でも，大好きな英語教育は私の生きがいでもあり，終生おつきあいさせていただくつもりです。

　この本が，全国の先生方の毎日の授業に少しでもお役に立つよう願ってやみません。また，この本をお使いいただいてのご意見やご感想をぜひお寄せください。お待ちしております。

2001年　夏

藤井　昌子

Afterword

Mrs Fujii and I hope that you and your students have enjoyed the activities in this book, and thank you for using it. Should you have any criticisms or other comments, please send them to us via the publisher. If you have any ideas of your own that you'd like to see included in any follow-up to this book, again, please post them to Kairyudo for consideration.

Enjoy your teaching!

Steven Ashton

August, 2001

執 筆 協 力 者

赤池　秀代	浦和明の星女子高等学校教諭
岸部千鶴子	埼玉県新座市立第六中学校教諭
北野　　晃	埼玉県入間市教育委員会指導主事
後藤　範子	埼玉県立菖蒲高等学校教諭
関口　　睦	埼玉県狭山市立西中学校教諭
中村　正美	埼玉県立大宮武蔵野高等学校教諭
成田也寸志	埼玉県久喜市立久喜南中学校教諭
深井　祐子	埼玉県草加市立新栄中学校教諭
本多　綾子	埼玉県立熊谷西高等学校教諭
本多みどり	愛知県岡崎市立六ツ美中学校教諭

（所属は執筆時のもの）

■著者紹介■

藤井　昌子（ふじい　まさこ）
　　　　東京国際大学・言語コミュニケーション学部非常勤講師
　　　　埼玉県下の高等学校の英語教師，外国語担当指導主事，教頭，校長を歴任し，平成18年3月，草加南高等学校長を最後に退職。財団法人語学教育研究所理事・パーマー賞選考委員。
　　　　主な著書：『言語活動成功事例集』『新・言語活動成功事例集』（開隆堂出版），『英語授業学の視点』（三省堂），授業ビデオ『文型・文法事項等導入法再検討』（ジャパンライム），以上共著／『「どうせ自分なんて」と，つぶやく君に』『忘れない 私の13,879日』（開隆堂出版）／『ヴィスタ英和辞典』（三省堂）執筆，他

スティーヴン・アシュトン（Steven Ashton）
　　　　ELEC（財団法人英語教育協議会）講師管理副部長
　　　　英国サセックス大学（物理学専攻）卒，インペリアル・カレッジ・ロンドン修士課程（工業経営学）修了。その後，ヨーロッパで財政業務に従事。平成9年に来日し，埼玉県教育委員会で3年間ALTを務める。平成12年に現職。ELECでは日本人英語教員へのトレーニングも含め，さまざまな英語研修の企画・運営を担当。また，日本の教育・文化的なテレビ番組，ドラマ，映画にも出演。ナレーター，声優，吹き替えなどもしている。
　　　　著書：『新・言語活動成功事例集』（共著，開隆堂出版）

日本語・英語解説による　続・言語活動成功事例集―Communication Activities

平成13年 8 月15日　　初版発行	
平成21年11月20日　　4 刷発行	
著　者　　藤井　昌子／スティーヴン・アシュトン	
発行者　　開隆堂出版株式会社　　〒113-8608 東京都文京区向丘1-13-1	
代表者　山　岸　忠　雄	
印刷所　　株式会社大熊整美堂　　〒112-0002 東京都文京区小石川4-14-32	
発行所　　開隆堂出版株式会社　　〒113-8608 東京都文京区向丘1-13-1	
電話　東京(03)5684-6115(編集)	
発売元　　開隆館出版販売株式会社　〒113-8608 東京都文京区向丘1-13-1	
電話　東京(03)5684-6121(営業)／6118(販売)	
振替　00100-5-55345　　URL：http://www.kairyudo.co.jp/	

表紙デザイン　クリエイティブスタジオ・ホワイトスペース(有)
本文イラスト　鈴木康代
ISBN978-4-304-01169-6 C3037　　　　　　　　落丁・乱丁本はお取り替えいたします。

コミュニケーション活動を成功させるためのヒントが満載

好評発売中！

日本語・英語解説による

新・言語活動成功事例集

第2章に長期スパンで取り組む活動を加え，さらに充実！

シリーズ待望の第3弾！

藤井 昌子
S・アシュトン
本多 綾子
　　　共著

■B5判／144ページ
■ワークシート・データCD-ROM付
■定価1,890円（本体1,800円）

新里眞男氏（東京国際大学教授）推薦！！

授業がマンネリになってきてパンチが欲しいとき，実際に習った表現を使って発話させたいとき，私はこの『事例集』を頼りにしてきました。第3弾の本書にも，初級から上級レベルまで使える日常的でコミュニカティブな活動例が満載です。また，今まで同様，コピーしてそのまま授業に持って行ける使い勝手のよさは非常に助かります。さらに，今回新設の「活動成功へのアドバイス」はベテラン教員ならではの味でしょう。第2章の「長期スパンで取り組む活動例」も加わり，英語教師の強い味方が増えたと言えます。

シリーズ第1弾
言語活動成功事例集
B5判／112ページ
定価1,000円（税込）
共著　藤井 昌子
　　　イヴァン・バーケル

シリーズ第2弾
続・言語活動成功事例集
B5判／124ページ
定価1,000円（税込）
共著　藤井 昌子
　　　スティーヴン・アシュトン

発行／開隆堂出版株式会社
発売／開隆館出版販売株式会社

〒113-8608 東京都文京区向丘1-13-1
電　話　03-5684-6118（販売）
振　替　00100-5-55345

身近な語彙・表現を補充して、コミュニケーション活動をパワーアップ！

好評発売中　中学・高校 英語副教材
B5判／48ページ／オールカラー
■定価500円（本体476円）

Let's Talk!

レッツ・トーク

これ 英語で
なんて言うの
！？

真尾正博　監修

二見隆久
鈴木浩明
伊藤幸男
宮本典行　共著

実践的コミュニケーション能力育成のサプリメント！

「実践的コミュニケーション能力」の育成を目指し様々な言語活動に取り組む。すぐに、「語彙不足」というストレスに生徒，教師ともに悩まされる。そんな不健康な状態から，ごく身近な雑談からある程度フォーマルなディスカッションまで，豊かにかつ細やかに自己表現できる健康な状態に回復・維持してくれるのが本書である。取り上げるトピックも自然であり，また，配列にも細かな配慮があり使い勝手がよい。さらに，しっかりとした理論に裏付けられた処方箋（解説）もあって安心できる。何より，長く使っていても飽きが来ない。まさに，本書は「実践的コミュニケーション能力育成のためのサプリメント」であると強く推薦する。
　　　　　　　　　　　　　青野 保（埼玉大学教育学部附属中学校 教諭）

教師用

『Let's Talk! 活用の手引き』
B5判／32ページ
■定価1,000円（本体952円）
（Let's Talk! テキスト1冊付き）

発行／開隆堂出版株式会社
発売／開隆館出版販売株式会社

〒113-8608 東京都文京区向丘1-13-1
電　話 03-5684-6118（販売）
振　替 00100-5-55345

イエス・ユー・キャン 1〜3年
〜言語活動ステップアップ事例集〜

好評発売中

石井利明，坂田三千代，青野亮子，山戸田孝則，笠井誠司，巽　徹　共著
各学年：B5判 80〜96頁 / 定価 各1,200円（本体1,143円）

　今や英語の授業は「コミュニケーション活動」真っ盛り。教師が黒板の前に立ちチョーク1本で行っていた，かつての一斉画一的授業風景とは，まさに隔世の感があります。生徒は生き生きとコミュニカティブ・アクティビティーを楽しんでいます。

　平成14年度から完全施行される新学習指導要領では，「ゲームやお遊び的コミュニケーション活動」から「実践的コミュニケーション活動」へと進化させていく必要性をうたっています。つまり「使える英語」の充実を提唱しているのです。そのためには「単発的な言語活動」から「テーマや目的をもった言語活動」が有効です。

- 中学校の英語教育現場で実証済みの優れた言語活動の指導事例を数多く紹介。
- 生徒が「できるようになる」シラバスを一挙に公開。
- ユニットごとに「できるようになること」を設定し，段階的にその目標が達成できる構成。
- 教師用の How To Use と生徒用のワークシートで構成。
- そのままコピーして授業に使えるワークシート。

できるようになること

■1年
- あいさつや自己紹介ができるようになる
- 家族・友だち・ペットを紹介できるようになる
- クリスマス・カードやポスターが作れるようになる
- スキットを作って上演できるようになる，など

■2年
- 日記が書けるようになる
- レストランで注文できるようになる
- 店員とやりとりしながら買い物ができるようになる
- 道案内できるようになる，など

■3年
- 名所・名物・特産物を紹介できるようになる
- 短いコマーシャルを作って発表できるようになる
- ディベートができるようになる
- 英字新聞の概要をつかめるようになる，など

発行／開隆堂出版株式会社
発売／開隆館出版販売株式会社

〒113-8608　東京都文京区向丘1-13-1
電　話　03-5684-6118（販売）
振　替　00100-5-55345